YOR]

General Ed
of Stirling)
University oj Deirui)

Charles Dickens

PICKWICK PAPERS

Notes by Michael Wheeler

MA (CAMBRIDGE) PH D (LONDON)
Lecturer in English Literature,
University of Lancaster

LONGMAN
YORK PRESS

YORK PRESS
Immeuble Esseily, Place Riad Solh, Beirut.

LONGMAN GROUP LIMITED
Burnt Mill,
Harlow, Essex

First published 1981
ISBN 0 582 78255 4

Printed in Hong Kong by
Sing Cheong Printing Co Ltd

Contents

Part 1

Introduction

His bright and joyful sympathy with everything around him; his steady practicality, withal; the singularly solid business talent he continually had; and, deeper than all, if one has the eye to see deep enough, dark, fateful, silent elements, tragical to look upon, and hiding, amid dazzling radiances as of the sun, the elements of death itself.

This is how Thomas Carlyle (1795-1881) sums up what he calls Dickens's 'manner of existing', in a letter of 1874 in which he congratulates John Forster on the publication of the third volume of his *Life of Charles Dickens*. Carlyle was looking back over a brilliant literary career of over thirty years, in which Dickens established himself as the most widely loved and respected novelist in an age of great novelists; and he saw that both Dickens and his works were essentially paradoxical in nature. Here was a novelist, probably the greatest in the English language, whose bright and joyful sympathy, evident in the portrayal of many of his characters and in his own love of good fellowship, made it possible for him to create distinct and complete imaginative worlds, entering the minds of an extraordinary range of characters and thus making them 'live'. Yet there was also a very dark side to Dickens, of 'fateful, silent elements, tragical to look upon'. His powerful will usually suppressed or at least controlled his painful sensitivity to the miseries of periods of his boyhood and early manhood, of his unhappy marriage, and of his growing sense in middle age that modern society reflected the very worst aspects of human selfishness and greed. This strong will often lashed him into frenzied activity, and eventually probably killed him.

The darker side of Dickens's vision is most clearly evident in his later and greatest novels. Although early signs of it are to be found in his first novel, *Pickwick Papers*, Carlyle's brighter epithets, like 'joyful' and 'dazzling', spring most readily to mind as we read the work which, after the publication of a few numbers, made its author famous virtually overnight. *Pickwick Papers* celebrates the noblest qualities of man, such as goodness and love, and affirms what Keats called 'the holiness of the heart's affections'. How did Dickens achieve this without becoming sententious or sentimental, as he sometimes did in weak passages of his later novels? How did he make goodness and warm-heartedness interesting, when evil characters and deeds usually enthral the readers of

literature more easily? And what is the relationship between the posi-
tive, life-affirming qualities of *Pickwick Papers* and the novel's darker
themes? These are some of the central critical questions which will be
raised in Part 3 of these Notes.

In Part 4 the reader will be shown how to select significant passages
from a long novel and to organise a critical argument related to this
selected material, when preparing an essay or answering an examination question. It is hoped, however, that these Notes will not only offer
guidance to the student of *Pickwick Papers*, but will also stimulate
further reading and critical analysis of the novel.

Life of Charles Dickens (1812–70)

Dickens was born on 7 February 1812 in Portsea, near Portsmouth. He
was the second of eight children born to John Dickens, a clerk in the
Navy Pay Office, and his wife Elizabeth, the daughter of a senior man
in the same office. John Dickens's work later took the family to Chatham
in Kent. Here Charles enjoyed the happiest days of his childhood, until
the age of nine, visiting the theatre, watching military parades, discovering the beauties of the countryside, and reading eighteenth-
century fiction and such classics as the *Arabian Nights*, which fed his
lively imagination. He also enjoyed two years in a school run by the
enlightened young son of a Baptist minister, who saw that the boy had
promise. It is hardly surprising that the area is often the setting for
episodes in his novels, including *Pickwick Papers*, and that he returned
there to live in later life.

When the family moved to Camden Town, a suburb of London,
young Charles's life took a turn for the worse. John Dickens's debts got
him into serious financial difficulties. So instead of going to school,
Charles helped around the house and ran errands, developing an acute
sense of alienation from the mean surroundings in which he now lived.
When his father was taken to the Marshalsea prison for debt in 1824,
the family moved in with him, except for Charles, who lived alone in
lodgings. He had already been found work in a blacking factory off the
Strand, labelling bottles of shoe polish, in order to supplement the
family's income. As an adult he could hardly bring himself to speak of
the 'grief and humiliation' of those long days of repetitive work, and of
the Sunday visits to the prison which was to be the most important
setting in *Little Dorrit*. Dickens's early observations of the debtors'
prison also provided him with material for the episodes in the Fleet
prison in *Pickwick Papers*, and for the Marshalsea setting of the tale of
the Queer Client (Chapter 21).

After three months' imprisonment, John Dickens inherited some
money from his mother, who was a retired housekeeper. Although the

bequest did not solve all his financial difficulties, he could at least leave the Marshalsea. Charles continued to work at the blacking factory for a while, and then went to a badly run private school for two years. In 1827 he became a lawyer's office-boy, and developed his lifelong interest in the theatre. During his time in the lawyer's office, Dickens taught himself shorthand. He then became a reporter, first in the court of Doctors' Commons, where he took down the details of numerous lengthy and usually tedious legal cases, and later in the gallery of the House of Commons, where he soon made a name for himself. In his early twenties he also covered political speeches around the country, travelling everywhere by coach in the age before the coming of the railways. All these experiences of early adulthood are reflected in *Pickwick Papers*. Dickens first fell in love with Maria Beadnell, a banker's daughter, at the age of seventeen. Although he courted her for several years, the gap which separated them socially, together with the coldness of Maria's family towards him, eventually proved fatal to the relationship.

Dickens's first literary efforts were short pieces for magazines and newspapers, and his *Sketches by Boz* were collected in two volumes in 1836. On 2 April of that year he married Catherine Hogarth, the eldest daughter of his journalist colleague George Hogarth, editor of the *Evening Chronicle*. The couple married on the prospect of a new venture: three days previously, the first number of *Pickwick Papers* had been published. After the appearance of the fourth monthly number, in which Hablot Browne took over from Seymour, the original illustrator, who had committed suicide, and in which the character of Sam Weller was first introduced, the novel became a huge success and had a large reading public eagerly awaiting the publication of subsequent numbers on the last day of each month. Halfway through the publication of *Pickwick*, Dickens began to write *Oliver Twist*, which appeared concurrently in the same monthly form. Dickens's son, Charley, the first of his ten children, was born in January 1837, the year in which Queen Victoria came to the throne. Publication of both *Pickwick* and *Oliver Twist* was briefly held up when Dickens's much loved sister-in-law, Mary Hogarth, who lived with Dickens's family, died suddenly in May 1837 at the age of seventeen. *Pickwick* darkens in the chapters describing the Fleet prison, written not long after this most shattering bereavement.

Dickens worked at a cracking pace during 1836 and 1837, when he was writing two serial novels, and was for some time heavily involved in journalistic enterprises, edited the memoirs of the famous clown Grimaldi, kept up his interest in amateur theatricals and London theatre-going, and enjoyed a busy social life. He certainly needed that 'solid business talent' and 'steady practicality' of which Carlyle wrote.

And the pace hardly slackened during the remainder of his working life. As successful novels were published in quick succession, *Nicholas Nickleby* (1838–9), *The Old Curiosity Shop* (1840–1) and *Barnaby Rudge* (1841), Dickens's circle of influential friends widened. He and his wife were warmly received in the United States during a visit which provided material for his *American Notes* (1842). *Martin Chuzzlewit* (1843–4) was not a popular success, although *A Christmas Carol* (1843) made up for that failure, being the first of Dickens's eagerly anticipated Christmas Books.

The years from 1846 to 1850 are a kind of bridge passage in Dickens's career, for in *Dombey and Son* (1846–8) and the partly autobiographical *David Copperfield* (1849–50), his handling of serious themes, and of symbolism and plot, matures. In 1850 he founded his own weekly family periodical, *Household Words*, which demanded yet more of his time and energy. It was succeeded by *All the Year Round* in 1859.

The novels which followed *David Copperfield* reflect Dickens's deepening concern with social issues. *Bleak House* (1852–3), possibly his greatest novel, and *Little Dorrit* (1855–7) brilliantly satirise the workings of the law and the bureaucracy of Victorian England. In the year between the publication of these novels, Dickens published *Hard Times* (1854), a vivid but highly stylised portrayal of life in a northern industrial town, in *Household Words*. By the time he published *A Tale of Two Cities* (1859), Dickens had separated from his wife and befriended the actress Ellen Ternan. *Great Expectations* (1860–1), today one of his most widely read works, and *Our Mutual Friend* (1864–5), one of his greatest achievements, were the last completed novels. The last years of his life were partly taken up with exhausting reading tours of Britain and America. Dickens drove himself hard in these readings of his own works, in order to satisfy his deep need for close contact with his public, which he felt had been slipping in the later years of his novel-writing career. He died of a stroke suffered after a full day's work on his last, unfinished novel, *Edwin Drood*, in June 1870. For days after his burial in Poets' Corner, Westminster Abbey, crowds of people gathered around the grave to pay their last respects to this extraordinary writer, the great showman, social critic, symbolist, and, perhaps above all, creator of the many hundreds of fascinating characters who inhabit the Dickens world.

Historical background

We need to read and study works of literature in their historical context. The first point to make about *Pickwick Papers* in this respect is that the novel is *pre*-Victorian. Published in 1836–7, the novel is set in 1827–8. (Notice, however, that Dickens often refers to events of the 1830s in

Pickwick.) This puts the action of the novel in the reign of George IV, between the Regency period (1811–20)—portrayed in Jane Austen's (1775–1817) novels and, later, in Thackeray's (1811–63) *Vanity Fair* (1847–8)—and the period of the Reform Act of 1832—in which George Eliot's (1819–80) *Middlemarch* (1871–2) is set. (It would be valuable to compare these writers' different portrayals of early nineteenth-century England.)

Although the Industrial Revolution which was to change the face of England by the end of the nineteenth century had begun in the north and the midlands in the last quarter of the previous century, we get only a brief glimpse of its effects in the Birmingham chapter (Chapter 50) in *Pickwick*. The 'landed interest' and the professions are as yet more influential than the up-and-coming industrialists, and the country's centre of gravity is firmly in the south, above all, of course, in London. In the age immediately preceding the coming of the railways, Pickwick and his friends travel by coach, and stay in the old coaching inns in country towns. Their outdoor country pursuits include cricket, skating and shooting. Indoors, whist, story-telling and convivial drinking are enjoyed in snug rooms by warm fires. The Pickwickians meet representatives of the clergy, the army, the medical profession and the country magistracy. In London, the legal profession appears to trap people from all levels of society in its web of inefficiency and dubious practices. (Dickens did not, however, fully develop his attack on the law until he wrote *Bleak House*, in which he related his view of it to the whole fabric of English society.) The Bardell-Pickwick case was based on the notorious Norton-Melbourne trial, reported at length by Dickens himself in the *Morning Chronicle* of 23 June 1836.

Just as we only glimpse Birmingham, the town that was rapidly becoming the workshop of the world, so we have no sense in *Pickwick* of the large urban working class in Dickens's later novels. Social divisions are certainly sharply defined, as we see early in the novel when Jingle tells Tupman that in Rochester, 'Dock-yard people of lower rank don't know small gentry—small gentry don't know tradespeople', and so on (Chapter 2). Although Dickens often portrays the snobbishness which has long been a national characteristic of the English, he shows us very little social conflict in *Pickwick*. At Dingley Dell, Sam Weller and Joe, the fat boy, naturally clear the ice before their 'betters' skate on it (Chapter 30). But notice how they are joined by their masters, Pickwick and Wardle, in an unselfconscious way, when they make a slide on the ice. Although it must always be borne in mind that we are presented with an idyllic view of country life in *Pickwick*, the novel does accurately reflect the comparative innocence of the old ways which were soon to be eroded in the Victorian age of rapid socio-economic change and expansion.

Literary background

The book which influenced Dickens's work more than any other was the Bible, and the ethics of *Pickwick*, as of his later novels, are firmly grounded in the New Testament. Stylistically, Dickens is original and unique. He developed a prose style which is lively and flexible, often rapidly changing from a simple narrative style to a highly mannered rhetoric of hyperbole, repetition and dramatic variations of tone. Dickens had been a journalist for some years before writing *Pickwick*, and had thus learnt to describe events briefly but interestingly, and to report speeches accurately. His regular theatre-going also influenced his novel-writing, both in style and in plotting.

In terms of more direct literary influence, two bodies of literature are of paramount importance. First, eighteenth-century fiction and, behind much of that fiction, *Don Quixote* (1605-15) by the Spanish author Miguel de Cervantes (1547-1616), which Dickens read avidly as a boy. Everybody who comments on Dickens's sources cites the famous paragraph in the first chapter of Forster's *Life of Charles Dickens*, in which he states that the following passage from the fourth chapter of *David Copperfield* was literally true of the young Dickens himself:

> My father had left a small collection of books in a little room upstairs, to which I had access (for it adjoined my own), and which nobody else in our house ever troubled. From that blessed little room, Roderick Random, Peregrine Pickle, Humphrey Clinker, Tom Jones, the Vicar of Wakefield, Don Quixote, Gil Blas, and Robinson Crusoe, came out, a glorious host, to keep me company. They kept alive my fancy, and my hope of something beyond that place and time—they, and the *Arabian Nights*, and the *Tales of the Genii*.

Pickwick Papers, with its five coaching tours, draws on the picaresque tradition of much of this fiction, and includes several mock-heroic episodes which draw on the comic scenes of Cervantes, the English novelist Henry Fielding (1707-54) and the Scottish novelist Tobias Smollett (1721-71). Steven Marcus makes very helpful comments on Dickens's debt to his eighteenth-century precursors, and points out that Dickens's is a gentler kind of humour than theirs.* He also claims that two particular novels are specific sources. R.S. Surtees's (1803-64) *Jorrocks' Jaunts and Jollities* (1831-4) was just the kind of sporting novel Dickens might have written instead of *Pickwick*, had he agreed to write his text specifically to accompany the plates of Seymour, his first illustrator. Pickwick owes something to Surtees's hero, but is more gently benevolent, and altogether less aggressive than the vulgar

*Steven Marcus, *Dickens: From Pickwick to Dombey*, Chatto and Windus, London, 1965, pp.20-30.

Jorrocks. The Irish writer Oliver Goldsmith's (1728-74) *The Vicar of Wakefield* (1766) is similar to *Pickwick* in that it becomes more serious in the course of the story, when the hero is imprisoned voluntarily.

The second body of literature which had a formative influence on Dickens is Romantic poetry, although here the effect of his reading on his writing is much vaguer. By 1825, Keats, Shelley and Byron were dead, and Wordsworth and Coleridge had long since produced their greatest poetry. In the 1830s this literary vacuum was only partially filled by experimental, tentative reappraisals of Romanticism by writers who were later to develop into major Victorian literary figures. Carlyle developed his Romantic ideas in his early essays and in *Sartor Resartus*. Alfred, Lord Tennyson's (1809-92) first volume of poems owed much to John Keats (1795-1821) and other Romantic poets, and Robert Browning's (1812-89) early work is influenced by Shelley (1792-1822). Dickens, whose first novels appeared in the late 1830s, was to be the greatest Romantic novelist of the Victorian age. The mature novels of Dickens are visionary and mythic works, the products of a powerful and original imagination. Pickwick himself is a mythic figure, in a special sense that will be explained later. We will also see that one of the crucial words in the novel is *feeling*, that keyword of Romanticism. It has been argued that Romantic poetry is more significant as a source of Victorian fiction than was the fiction of the previous century.*

A note on the text

Pickwick Papers was first published in twenty parts as nineteen monthly numbers, from April 1836 to November 1837, the last number being a double issue. The full title was *The Posthumous Papers of the Pickwick Club: Containing a Faithful Record of the Perambulations, Perils, Travels, Adventures and Sporting Transactions of the Corresponding Members*, edited by Boz. The main editions in book form, each of which had a new preface by Dickens, were those of November 1837, printed from the plates of the numbers, the Cheap Edition of 1847, and the Charles Dickens Edition of 1867. Only fragments of the manuscript survive.

Of the modern editions (for instance the New Oxford Illustrated, Everyman, and Signet Classics) the most useful is the paperback Penguin English Library *Pickwick Papers*, edited by Robert L. Patten, Penguin Books, Harmondsworth, 1972, which is the edition referred to in these Notes. Patten takes the 1867 edition as his copy-text, and adds useful notes, many of which have been helpful in the preparation of the notes and glossaries appended to the chapter summaries in

*See John Speirs, *Poetry towards Novel*, Faber, London, 1971, pp.287-93, *et passim*.

Part 2. Patten prints Dickens's various prefaces to the novel, and all the illustrations by Seymour, Buss, and Hablot Browne, the illustrator from No. IV onwards. He also supplies a critical introduction and two maps.

Longman publish a simplified and abridged version of *Pickwick* in their Simplified English Series.

Summaries
of PICKWICK PAPERS

A general summary

(Note: the monthly numbers are indicated by roman numerals.)

(I) In May 1827, Samuel Pickwick sets off on his first tour with the three younger members of the Corresponding Society of the Pickwick Club: Tracy Tupman, Augustus Snodgrass and Nathaniel Winkle. (Pickwick's tours, as he explains in Chapter 57, at the end of the novel, allow him to mix 'with different varieties and shades of human character'.) They travel to Rochester by coach with Mr Jingle, a talkative itinerant actor, who proves to be extremely troublesome. His behaviour at a ball almost gets the innocent Winkle involved in a duel with Dr Slammer. (II) The first of the nine tales introduced in the course of the novel is 'The Stroller's Tale', told by a friend of Jingle's. The Pickwickians are caught up in a military review, but find safety in the carriage of one of Tupman's friends, Mr Wardle. They then have a series of accidents on their journey to Wardle's house at Dingley Dell, but (III) enjoy his hospitality when they arrive. Winkle proves that he cannot shoot, and Dingley Dell play the neighbouring town at cricket. Jingle is at the match. He soon spoils Tupman's chances of winning the affections of Wardle's sister, and (IV) elopes with her himself. Pickwick and Wardle follow the couple to London, where Pickwick meets Sam Weller, who is 'boots' at an inn, and Mr Perker, the lawyer, bribes Jingle to leave Miss Wardle alone. The Pickwickians follow the supposedly heartbroken Tupman to Cobham, Kent, where Pickwick makes what he wrongly considers to be an exciting antiquarian discovery. (V) Back in London, Pickwick's landlady, Mrs Bardell, mistakenly thinks he is proposing marriage to her, and faints in his arms. Sam Weller becomes Pickwick's servant.

The Pickwickians' second tour takes them to Eatanswill (based on the town of Sudbury, in Suffolk), where they witness the victory of the 'Blues' in a parliamentary election. (VI) The Pickwickians also attend Mrs Leo Hunter's literary 'breakfast', where they find Jingle masquerading under an assumed name. Pickwick and Sam follow Jingle to Bury St Edmunds, where Jingle and his servant, Job Trotter, escape from them by getting the innocent Pickwick into trouble at a local boarding-school for girls. (VII) Mrs Bardell issues a writ against Pickwick for a breach of promise of marriage. While his friends are partridge-shooting,

Pickwick falls asleep in a wheelbarrow on Captain Boldwig's land, and is placed in the village pound. He and Sam report to Mrs Bardell's London lawyers, Dodson and Fogg, and find Perker's clerk, Mr Lowten, in a public house.

(VIII) The third tour takes Sam and Pickwick to Ipswich in search of Jingle. Pickwick unfortunately mistakes the room of a Miss Witherfield for his own at an inn. Sam plans to have his revenge on Jingle and Job Trotter. (IX) Miss Witherfield thinks that her intended husband, Mr Magnus, might have a duel with Pickwick, and has Pickwick arrested. Nupkins, the mayor of Ipswich, releases Pickwick when the latter exposes Jingle as an impostor who has been living in Nupkins's own house. Having returned to London with Pickwick and his friends, Sam hears about Dodson's and Fogg's sharp practices. (X) He then visits the public house in Dorking run by his father, Tony, and the second Mrs Weller, who regularly entertains the hypocritical Reverend Mr Stiggins, the deputy Methodist minister. Sam and the Pickwickians spend a festive Christmas at Dingley Dell, where Mr Trundle and Bella Wardle are married. (XI) Two medical students, Bob Sawyer and Ben, the brother of the black-eyed Arabella Allen, join the company. Pickwick falls through the ice while skating. He and Sam return to their London lodgings in the George and Vulture, and meet the lawyers who are to defend him in the forthcoming trial. When Bob Sawyer entertains the Pickwickians at his lodgings, he is harassed by his landlady, Mrs Raddle. (XII) Sam writes a 'valentine' to Mary, Mayor Nupkins's housemaid, and accompanies his father to a temperance meeting attended by Mr Stiggins, which breaks up in disorder. In the trial of Bardell against Pickwick, Serjeant Buzfuz presents a false but successful prosecution case against Pickwick, who informs Dodson and Fogg that he would rather go to prison than pay any costs or damages.

(XIII) Pickwick and his friends make their fourth tour, this time to Bath, as Pickwick cannot be arrested for non-payment before two months have passed. Winkle is falsely accused of trying to elope with the wife of Mr Dowler, a fierce ex-army man, and escapes to Bristol. Sam attends a soirée of Bath footmen. (XIV) He then travels to Bristol in pursuit of Winkle, who has discovered that Bob Sawyer and Ben Allen have a medical practice there. Pickwick himself arrives, and joins Sam and Mary, now housemaid to a family who have moved to Clifton, in helping Winkle in his secret courtship of Arabella Allen, who is living with an aunt. The Pickwickians return to London, where Pickwick is arrested and taken to the Fleet, a debtors' prison.

(XV) Pickwick is deeply moved by what he sees in the Fleet, but also encounters a number of boisterous prisoners. He discovers the now destitute Jingle and Job Trotter in the 'poor side' of the prison, and gives them money. The loyal Sam persuades his father to have him arrested for debt so that Pickwick cannot make him leave the Fleet. (XVI) Master and servant are visited by Tupman, Snodgrass and Winkle, and then by Tony and Mrs Weller, and Stiggins. After a full tour of the prison, Pickwick decides to stay in his room in future. Mrs Bardell is herself imprisoned for debt, having been tricked by Dodson and Fogg. (XVII) Perker now points out to Pickwick that he should pay his own costs and those of Mrs Bardell in order to save her from hardship. Winkle arrives with Arabella, whom he has married after an elopement. He implores Pickwick to leave prison in order to explain matters to Ben Allen and Mr Winkle senior on his behalf. Pickwick agrees, leaves the Fleet, and starts on his fifth tour.

He travels first to Bristol, where he soothes the tempers of Ben, his aunt, and Bob Sawyer, Winkle's rival suitor, and then (XVIII) to Birmingham, accompanied by Sam, Ben and Bob, where Winkle's father declares that he will have no more to do with his son. On their return to London, Sam hears that his step-mother is dead and goes down to Dorking, where his father kicks Stiggins into the street and gives him a ducking.

(XIX–XX) Pickwick has instructed Perker to arrange for money to be provided for Jingle's and Job Trotter's release, and their passage to the West Indies. Wardle at first angrily refuses Snodgrass permission to marry his daughter, Emily, but his attitude towards them soon softens. Sam helps his father to sell his business and to get probate of his wife's will. Mr Winkle comes down from Birmingham and forgives his son and Arabella.

The novel ends in the late autumn of 1828, with Pickwick announcing the dissolution of the Pickwick Club and his own retirement to a house in Dulwich, from which Snodgrass and Emily Wardle are married. Sam remains Pickwick's faithful servant for two years, and then marries Mary, who becomes the housekeeper at Dulwich. Finally, the future lives of other characters in the novel are briefly outlined.

Detailed summaries

Chapter 1: The Pickwickians

Dickens, as 'editor', introduces the minutes of a meeting of the Pickwick Club in May 1827, recorded in the Club's Transactions, in which it is proposed that a Corresponding Society be established within the Club. Mr Samuel Pickwick and three other members, namely Tracy Tupman, ever susceptible to love, the poetic Augustus Snodgrass, and Nathaniel Winkle, the sportsman, are to further the pseudo-scientific aims of the London-based Club by travelling through England and submitting papers (hence the novel's title) on their observations and adventures.

NOTES AND GLOSSARY:

Tittlebats: childish variant of 'stickleback', a small fish

Hornsey . . . Camberwell: locations on the outskirts of London

was his Swing: set him on fire. 'Captain Swing' was a pseudonym of farm workers who threatened to burn ricks in protest against the introduction of machinery in the early 1830s. Note that numerous references in the novel are to events which occurred after 1827–8, the years in which it is set

humbug: impostor

Chapter 2: The first Day's Journey, and the first Evening's Adventures; with their Consequences

---

Setting out in a cab the following day, Pickwick is mistaken for an informer by the driver, who starts a fight. The Pickwickians are rescued by the loquacious Mr Jingle, and accompany him by coach to Rochester in Kent. Tupman attends a charity ball with Jingle, who borrows Winkle's dress suit without his knowledge. Jingle dances with a wealthy widow, thus angering Dr Slammer, an army surgeon. Next morning Slammer sends a challenge to the owner of the suit, the innocent Winkle, but stops the duel when he sees that Winkle is not the man who offended him.

NOTES AND GLOSSARY:

waterman: attendant who waters horses

jemmy: (*slang*) coat

pig's whisper: (*slang*) short period of time

somebody else's head: that of King Charles I, executed in 1649

through the button-hole: bottles were passed to the left, the side on which men had their button-holes

heeltaps: liquor left in a glass

Bacchus: Greek god of wine

nobs: (*slang*) members of the upper classes

Alexander Selkirks: Selkirk (1676–1721) of Largo, in Fife, Scotland, was a buccaneer, who at his own request was put ashore on Juan Fernandez where he lived alone for four years and four months. Daniel Defoe (1660–1731) based his *Robinson Crusoe* (1719) on Selkirk, and William Cowper's (1731–1800) poem on him begins, 'I am monarch of all I survey'

Twopenny: refers to the postal rate

satisfaction pistols: duelling pistols, with which honour could be satisfied

Chapter 3: A new Acquaintance. The Stroller's Tale. A disagreeable Interruption, and an unpleasant Encounter

Jingle, himself an itinerant actor, has introduced another 'stroller' to the Pickwickians—Jem Hutley. 'Dismal Jemmy' tells the tale of the 'progress downwards' of a low pantomime actor, whose addiction to drink led to *delirium tremens* and a terrible death. Dr Slammer and his friends arrive, and Tupman and Jingle are recognised. A duel is again averted, however, when the doctor's haughty friends point out that Jingle is not a gentleman, and therefore cannot be challenged.

NOTES AND GLOSSARY:

surtout: overcoat
drab: cloth of a dull, light-brown colour
running . . . to seed: becoming shabby, worn
black-eyed Susan: Douglas Jerrold's melodrama, *Black-eyed Susan; or, All in the Downs* (1829), based on a famous song in *The Beggar's Opera* (1728) by John Gay (1685–1732), is the source of Jingle's pun on Jemmy's state of mind—down, depressed
tumblers: acrobats
Dance of Death: in Hans Holbein's (1497–1543) sequence of wood-cuts the skeletal figure of Death moves among the living

Chapter 4: A Field-Day and Bivouac. More new Friends. An Invitation to the Country

Next morning, Pickwick, Winkle and Snodgrass are accidentally caught up in a mock battle at a military review, but find safety in the carriage of Mr Wardle, a friend of Tupman's. They are served a picnic meal by Joe, the fat boy, who rouses himself from sleep only to eat. Tupman flirts with Wardle's sister, Rachael. Wardle invites the Pickwickians to his home, Manor Farm, at Dingley Dell.

NOTES AND GLOSSARY:

Bivouac: a temporary encampment of troops in the field, here for a public review
New River Head: where London's water-supply originally ended
the Lines: large parade ground next to Chatham barracks
glazed stocks: stiff band around the neck, usually of leather
sally-port: opening in a fortification from which besieged troops could attack besiegers
barouche: a four-wheeled carriage

Chapter 5: A short one. Showing, among other Matters, how Mr Pickwick undertook to drive, and Mr Winkle to ride; and how they both did it

Before breakfast the following morning, Pickwick has a brief discussion with Dismal Jemmy, the stroller, who promises to send him a 'curious manuscript'. Pickwick's and Winkle's lack of skill with horses leads to a series of accidents on the road to Dingley Dell in which the Pickwickians' bodies are less seriously injured than is their pride. They walk dejectedly to Manor Farm, where Wardle's warm hospitality contrasts with the treatment they received from an unnamed couple on their way there.

NOTES AND GLOSSARY:
balmy: mild, soothing
hostler: stableman at an inn
quickset: hedge formed of living ('quick') plants, often hawthorn
t'ant: it is not
blunderbuss: ancient type of large-bore gun

Chapter 6: An old-fashioned Card-party. The Clergyman's Verses. The Story of the Convict's Return

The Pickwickians are introduced to the company in the old parlour at Manor Farm. Tupman continues his flirtation with Wardle's sister during a lively game of cards. After supper the party sits round the fire and listens to the clergyman's tale of 'The Convict's Return'. This tells of the dreadful suffering of a local woman who was tormented by her drunkard husband and later abandoned by her son. The son becomes a criminal and is transported for fourteen years. Not knowing that his mother has died, the penitent convict returns to Dingley Dell at the end of his sentence, only to find that the old family house has new occupants. He meets his impoverished father by chance, and the old man dies when a blood-vessel bursts during the encounter.

NOTES AND GLOSSARY:
brought up in the way she should go . . .: see the Bible, Proverbs 22:6
samplers: specimens of embroidery on canvas or other material
Ripstone-pippin-faced: Ribstone pippin is a variety of apple
rubber: best of three games at whist
Pope Joan: popular card game played on a special board
the rub: that is, the rubber is won
sotted: got drunk
workhouse: house for the poor

Chapter 7: How Mr Winkle, instead of shooting at the Pigeon and killing the Crow, shot at the Crow and wounded the Pigeon; how the Dingley Dell Cricket Club played All-Muggleton, and how All-Muggleton dined at the Dingley Dell expense: with other interesting and instructive Matters

Next morning the idyllic peace of the countryside is broken when Wardle takes Winkle out to shoot rooks. It turns out that Winkle has fostered a false reputation as a sportsman, much to Pickwick's displeasure. He misses the rooks but hits Tupman, injuring him only slightly and giving Miss Wardle a chance to make a great fuss of him. While Tupman recovers with the ladies, his fellow Pickwickians leave for a cricket match at the neighbouring town of Muggleton. Jingle is there, enjoying the occasion. Although Dingley Dell lose the match, both sides join in the festivities which follow with great enthusiasm.

NOTES AND GLOSSARY:

cows on the chimney-pots: cow is a Kentish dialect variant of cowl, a kind of cover

stone crop: a low, creeping plant which often grows on walls

the infant Lambert: Joe. Daniel Lambert weighed fifty-three stone (742 pounds) at his death in 1809 at Stamford

corn-factor's: grain-dealer

marquee: large tent

an entry of a song: by the dramatist John O'Keefe (1747–1833)

cold, without: of spirits—cold, without water

Chapter 8: Strongly illustrative of the Position, that the Course of True Love is not a Railway

Back at Manor Farm, Joe sees Tupman kissing Miss Wardle in the arbour (see note below). The cricket party arrives home drunk after midnight. Next morning, Jingle overhears Joe telling old Mrs Wardle about her daughter and Tupman. Jingle, himself interested in Miss Wardle's money, hatches a plot whereby she is made to believe that he truly loves her, whereas Tupman only wants her money and actually loves her niece, Emily, of whom she has long been jealous.

NOTES AND GLOSSARY:

the Course of True Love . . .: 'The course of true love never did run smooth', from Shakespeare's *A Midsummer Night's Dream*, I.1.134

arbour: a shady retreat, part of a garden

blanc-mange: a kind of milk jelly

suffered him: allowed him

independence:	independent income
Fielding:	John Wade (1788–1875), under the pseudonym 'Thomas Fielding', included the proverb in his *Select Proverbs of all Nations* (1824)
tow:	the (inflammable) fibre of flax, hemp, or jute

Chapter 9: A Discovery and a Chase

Jingle elopes with Miss Wardle, causing confusion and uproar among the company at Manor Farm. Wardle and Pickwick follow in hot pursuit, both couples covering the 'stages' on the highway in a series of fast hired coaches. Just as the pursuers catch up with Jingle, their coach crashes and they are forced to continue on foot.

NOTES AND GLOSSARY:

gig:	light, two-wheeled, one-horse carriage
chaise and four:	a larger vehicle, here a four-wheeled coach drawn by four horses
post-boy . . . leader . . . wheeler:	there are two postilions driving, one sitting on the leading left-hand horse, the other on the left-hand horse nearest the wheels

Chapter 10: Clearing up all Doubts (if any existed) of the Disinterestedness of Mr Jingle's Character

Jingle and Miss Wardle have arrived in London and are staying at a coaching inn, the White Hart at Southwark. Sam Weller, the 'boots', explains some of the mysteries of the law courts, and Jingle goes to get a special marriage licence. Wardle and Pickwick arrive at the inn with a lawyer, Mr Perker, who bribes Jingle to leave, on the grounds that he is interested only in Miss Wardle's money anyway. Wardle and Pickwick take Miss Wardle home to Dingley Dell.

NOTES AND GLOSSARY:

the Borough:	that is, the Borough of Southwark, on the Surrey (south) side of the Thames
Jack Ketch:	an executioner (*d.* 1686) whose name was later applied to hangmen
Mr Warren . . . Day and Martin:	rival manufacturers of shoe blacking. Dickens himself worked at Warren's as a boy
Doctors' Commons:	law courts for cases concerning matrimony and legacies, among other things
Old Bailey:	major criminal court in London
Proctors:	lawyers who handled cases in civil or canon law

blunt: (*slang*) money
Belle Savage: a coaching inn at the bottom of Ludgate Hill
Markis o' Granby: many English inns were named after the Marquess of Granby (1721–70)
'In hurry, poste-haste. . . .': the opening lines of a song in Kane O'Hara's (1722–82) play *Tom Thumb*, an adaptation of Henry Fielding's burlesque
amicus curiae: (*Latin*) friend of the court
ad captandum: (*Latin*) bribe
Barnwell: Perker refers to R.V. Barnewall's legal reports (1817–34), but Pickwick thinks he means George Barnwell of the play of that name (1731) by George Lillo (1693–1739)
Gray's Inn: one of the Inns of Court
lucky: (*slang*) escape

Chapter 11: Involving another Journey, and an Antiquarian Discovery. Recording Mr Pickwick's Determination to be present at an Election; and containing a Manuscript of the old Clergyman's

---

Next day, Pickwick, Snodgrass and Winkle leave Manor Farm to follow the supposedly broken-hearted Tupman to Cobham, Kent, where he soon recovers. Pickwick finds a stone on which an ancient inscription appears to be written. During a restless night, he reads the horrifying 'Madman's Manuscript' which the clergyman at Dingley Dell gave him. This purports to be written by a madman who tried to murder both his wife, who married him for his money, and her brother, who planned the match. Having returned to London with his friends, Pickwick prepares for their forthcoming trip to Eatanswill, in Suffolk, and lectures to the Club on the inscription. In the ensuing controversy, the many learned societies which acclaim Pickwick's discovery refuse to recognise Mr Blotton's sound evidence that the inscription was written by the cottager, Bill Stumps, from whom Pickwick bought it.

NOTES AND GLOSSARY:
porter's knot: a protective pad, sometimes of knotted rope, worn over the back and shoulders of a porter when carrying a heavy load

---

Chapter 12: Descriptive of a very important Proceeding on the Part of Mr Pickwick; no less an Epoch in his Life, than in this History

---

Pickwick's London landlady, Mrs Bardell, mistakenly thinks that he is proposing marriage to her, and faints in his arms. His friends are

suspicious when they find the couple in what seems to be an embrace.
Sam Weller is summoned from Southwark, agrees to be Pickwick's
servant, and sets off for Eatanswill with the Pickwickians the following
morning.

NOTES AND GLOSSARY:
farden: farthing, worth one quarter of an old penny

Chapter 13: Some Account of Eatanswill; of the State of Parties therein; and of the Election of a Member to serve in Parliament for that ancient, loyal, and patriotic Borough

---

The Pickwickians find that everything in Eatanswill is divided on party
lines. They drift into the 'Blue' side in the election, but only because
Pickwick knows Perker, who is acting as agent for the Honourable
Samuel Slumkey, the Blue candidate. Winkle flirts with the wife of Mr
Pott, the Blue newspaper editor. The innocent Pickwick is horrified to
see bribery and corruption going on openly in the town, but Sam Weller
assures him that this is usual at elections. After unruly scenes which
suggest that the town is well named, Slumkey is returned to parliament
as the member for Eatanswill.

NOTES AND GLOSSARY:
schedules A and B: the two forms of return for income tax assessment
the Blues and the Buffs: these colours have been associated with different ent parties at various times, the Tories generally having had blue favours, the Whigs blue and buff, a dull yellow. Blue usually signified support for the 'old interest', buff or yellow for the 'new'
fugleman: a leader in military drill, or, as here, the leader of a crowd
ecarté: a card game for two players
half baptized: a special Order of Baptism can be read for dangerously ill babies at home
choleric: angry

Chapter 14: Comprising a brief Description of the Company at the Peacock assembled; and a Tale told by a Bagman

---

Tupman and Snodgrass are staying at the Peacock inn at Eatanswill,
and listen to a tale told by a one-eyed bagman, or commercial traveller.
Tom Smart, himself a bagman in the previous century, stays at a country
inn one stormy night. An old chair in his bedroom takes on the appearance of an old man, who tells Tom that he will marry the widowed

landlady of the inn, having first exposed her present suitor as a married man with children. The chair's wishes are fulfilled.

NOTES AND GLOSSARY:

watch-box:	small shelter, similar to a sentry-box, used by watchmen
driving-boxes:	coachmen's boxes, containing their own belongings
imperence:	(*slang*) impertinence
Dutch pipe:	clay 'churchwarden' pipe, with a long stem
basket buttons:	metal buttons stamped with a basket-work pattern

Chapter 15: In which is given a faithful Portraiture of two distinguished Persons; and an accurate Description of a Public Breakfast in their House and Grounds: which Public Breakfast leads to the Recognition of an old Acquaintance, and the commencement of another Chapter

The Pickwickians are invited to a fancy-dress reception for literary celebrities, or 'lions', at 'The Den', Eatanswill, home of the aptly named Mrs Leo Hunter. Once a dispute between Pickwick and Tupman has been settled, the friends choose suitable costumes and drive to the 'breakfast'. Jingle is there under an assumed name, and hurries off when he is recognised. Pickwick and Sam Weller set off for Bury St Edmunds in pursuit of the man they want to expose as a fraud.

NOTES AND GLOSSARY:

Doctor Faustus:	at the end of Christopher Marlowe's (1564–93) play *Dr Faustus*, devils drag him off to hell
fête champêtre:	(*French*) rustic celebration, rural party
'feasts of reason . . .':	in fact from Alexander Pope's (1688–1744) *Imitations of Horace*, Book II, Satire I, line 128. Quintus Horatius Flaccus (65–8BC) was a Roman poet and satirist
Minerva:	Roman goddess of poetry and other arts; she was also associated with the Greek goddess Athene and was thus also known as the goddess of war
knout:	Russian whip
Baker's patent:	trade name of a patented mangle

Chapter 16: Too full of Adventure to be briefly described

During the journey to Bury, Sam tells Pickwick about his past. They stay at the Angel inn, where Jingle and his servant, Job Trotter, are lodged. Next day, Job puts Pickwick and Sam off Jingle's scent by telling them that his master is planning to elope with a girl from a local boarding-school. That night, Pickwick is taken for an intruder in the school, but is rescued by Sam, together with Mr Wardle and his destined son-in-law, Mr Trundle, who have arrived in Bury. Meanwhile Job and Jingle make their escape from the town.

NOTES AND GLOSSARY:

mother-in-law: here, step-mother

Right as a trivet: perfectly all right. A trivet is a firmly standing iron tripod for holding cooking vessels over a fire

British Hollands: gin, originally introduced from Holland

Chapter 17: Showing that an Attack of Rheumatism, in some cases, acts as a Quickener to Inventive Genius

Confined to bed with rheumatism, Pickwick writes the tale of 'The Parish Clerk', based on a story told him by Sam. The small and humble Nathaniel Pipkin falls in love with Maria Lobbs, daughter of a wealthy saddler. Maria and her cousins tease Nathaniel. In the end, however, he makes friends with old Lobbs, and accepts the fact that Maria loves her male cousin, whom she marries.

NOTES AND GLOSSARY:

parish clerk: a layman who had certain official duties, such as teaching, in a parish

Chapter 18: Briefly illustrative of two Points;—first, the Power of Hysterics, and, secondly, the Force of Circumstances

Meanwhile, back at Eatanswill, Winkle is glad to leave the Potts's house when some verse is printed in the 'Buffs'' newspaper which draws attention to his flirtation with Mrs Pott. The Pickwickians rejoin their leader in Bury, where Wardle invites them all to Dingley Dell for Christmas and a family wedding. Pickwick hears that Mrs Bardell has issued a writ against him for a breach of promise of marriage.

Chapter 19: A pleasant Day, with an unpleasant Termination

Wardle takes Winkle and Tupman partridge-shooting, accompanied by the lame Pickwick in a wheelbarrow, pushed by Sam. Winkle again demonstrates his lack of skill with a gun. After lunch, Pickwick is left alone, asleep in the barrow. The fierce little owner of the land, Captain Boldwig, happens to be passing, and has Pickwick placed in the village pound, still asleep. On waking up, Pickwick is abused by the villagers, but is rescued by Wardle and Sam.

NOTES AND GLOSSARY:

covey:	a brood of partridges
rattan:	a kind of cane
spring guns:	poachers were deterred by concealed guns attached to trip wires
Punch ... Devil:	Punch defeats even the Devil in the traditional puppet show of Punch and Judy

---

Chapter 20: Showing how Dodson and Fogg were Men of Business, and their Clerks Men of Pleasure; and how an Affecting Interview took place between Mr Weller and his long-lost Parent; showing also what Choice Spirits assembled at the Magpie and Stump, and what a capital Chapter the next one will be

---

Pickwick and Sam report to Mrs Bardell's London lawyers, whose clerks' conversation reveals sharp practice in the profession. Pickwick loses his temper with the solicitors, but is hurried away by Sam, thus avoiding further trouble with the law. By chance, they meet Sam's father, an old coachman, who tells them that Jingle is in Ipswich, in Suffolk. Pickwick wants Mr Perker to act for him in the Bardell case, and finds the lawyer's clerk, Mr Lowten, in a public house.

NOTES AND GLOSSARY:

pomatum:	scented ointment for the hair
Seidlitz powder:	a laxative
drabs:	dull-coloured breeches
bluchers:	low boots
Temple:	the Inner and the Middle Temples are Inns of Court in the City of London
praecipe **book:**	book containing writs which are needed in order to initiate legal action
Dantzic spruce:	spruce beer
Mosaic studs:	shirt studs made of mosaic gold, a cheap brass alloy

---

Chapter 21: In which the Old Man launches forth into his favourite Theme, and relates a Story about a queer Client

---

One of Mr Lowten's companions at the Magpie and Stump, old Jack Bamber, relates some morbid anecdotes concerning past tenants of rooms in the old Inns of Court. He then tells the tale of an imprisoned debtor, called Heyling, who swears to avenge the death of his wife and son, indirectly caused by his father-in-law. First he lets the old man's only son drown as they both look on. He then ruins his father-in-law, and finally destroys him, using the law as a weapon.

Chapter 22: Mr Pickwick journeys to Ipswich, and meets with a romantic Adventure with a middle-aged Lady in Yellow Curl Papers

Tony Weller tells Sam about his wife's Methodism. He then drives Pickwick to Ipswich in search of Jingle. Mr Peter Magnus is also travelling there, to make a proposal of marriage. That night, at the Great White Horse inn, Pickwick unfortunately mistakes the room of a lady for his own, and has to make an undignified exit.

NOTES AND GLOSSARY:

new birth: When Nicodemus asked, 'How can a man be born when he is old?', Jesus answered, 'Except a man be born of water and of the Spirit, he cannot enter into the Kingdom of God' (see the Bible, John 3:4–5)

wessel of wrath: 'What if God, willing to shew his wrath, and to make his power known, endured with much long-suffering the vessels of wrath fitted to destruction' (see the Bible, Romans 9.22). Like his son, Tony Weller pronounces 'v' as 'w'

Afternoon: those lawyers created 'Serjeants-at-Law' of the Court of Common Pleas after Serjeant Thomas Noon Talfourd, to whom *Pickwick* was dedicated, were known as 'afternoons'

japanned: lacquered with a dark varnish

Blunderbore: giant in the nursery tale, 'Jack the Giant-killer'

Chapter 23: In which Mr Samuel Weller begins to devote his Energies to the Return Match between himself and Mr Trotter

Tony Weller returns to London, having encouraged Sam to restore the good family name by getting his own back on Job Trotter. Sam happens to meet Job, who slily suggests that he has good intentions and considers Jingle to be a bad man. Sam tells Pickwick of his plan of action.

NOTES AND GLOSSARY:

the number four collection: possibly the fourth volume (*Moral Songs*, 1730) of hymns by Isaac Watts (1674–1748)

Chapter 24: Wherein Mr Peter Magnus grows jealous, and the middle-aged Lady apprehensive, which brings the Pickwickians within the grasp of the Law

Mr Magnus proposes to and is accepted by Miss Witherfield, the lady whose room Pickwick mistook for his own. When she and Pickwick are introduced, both register horror and surprise, but refuse to explain matters to the jealous Magnus. Thinking that Magnus and Pickwick might have a duel, Miss Witherfield goes to Mr Nupkins, the mayor and principal magistrate of Ipswich. Nupkins has Pickwick and Tupman arrested by his special constables, led by old Mr Grummer. The prisoners are carried through the streets in a sedan chair. When Sam hits Grummer, he too is arrested.

NOTES AND GLOSSARY:
Your wash-up: Your worship. Dickens thus indicates Grummer's strong Suffolk accent

---

Chapter 25: Showing, among a variety of pleasant Matters, how majestic and impartial Mr Nupkins was; and how Mr Weller returned Mr Job Trotter's Shuttlecock as heavily as it came. With another Matter, which will be found in its Place

---

The angry and tyrannical Nupkins, aided by his more knowledgeable clerk, Jinks, hears the case against Pickwick and Tupman, and decides to demand bail. On Sam's advice, however, Pickwick persuades Nupkins to let them off, by indicating that he is harbouring an impostor, Jingle, who is now a friend of Mrs and Miss Nupkins. Pickwick and Sam fulfil their duty by publicly confronting Jingle and Job Trotter and exposing them. Before leaving, Sam kisses the Nupkins's pretty housemaid, twice.

NOTES AND GLOSSARY:
American aloe: a species of agave plant, not actually an aloe
gambooge tops: gamboge is a resin used to make a bright yellow pigment, here applied to top-boots
Newgate Calendar: popular publication containing the life stories of notorious criminals
Mr Perceval: Spencer Perceval, the British Prime Minister, was assassinated in 1812 by an insane man who bore him a grudge
Saugur Point: on Saugur Island in the Bay of Bengal

Chapter 26: Which contains a brief Account of the Progress of the Action of Bardell against Pickwick

---

Next day, Pickwick and his friends return to London, where they separate to prepare for their Christmas visit to Dingley Dell. Sam visits Mrs Bardell on the pretext of paying the rent and making arrangements for the removal of Pickwick's belongings. He learns from her and her two friends that the case against Pickwick is to be heard in February or March, and that Dodson and Fogg, Mrs Bardell's lawyers, will be resorting to sharp practice as usual.

NOTES AND GLOSSARY:
flat candle: a candle in a candlestick with a flat base

Chapter 27: Samuel Weller makes a Pilgrimage to Dorking, and beholds his Mother-in-law

---

Sam visits the Marquis of Granby public house in Dorking, Surrey, where he meets his sharp-tongued step-mother for the first time. She is not pleased to see him, as she is enjoying the company of the hypocritical Reverend Mr Stiggins, deputy minister (or 'shepherd') at the Methodist chapel, who virtually lives off her. Tony Weller arrives home and takes comfort from Sam's sympathy. Sam leaves next morning, having advised his father to drop Stiggins in the water-butt.

NOTES AND GLOSSARY:
quondam relict and sole executrix: legal terminology for the former widow who was the only person nominated by her husband to 'execute' his will
It's all vanity: 'Vanity of vanities, saith the Preacher, vanity of vanities; all is vanity' (see the Bible, Ecclesiastes 1:2)
A man of wrath: 'A man of great wrath shall suffer punishment' (see the Bible, Proverbs 19:19)
the nails in the horse's shoes: arithmetical problem in which a horse is sold for a sum calculated by doubling the previous figure for each horseshoe nail, starting with a farthing
Walker: the exclamation 'Walker!' or 'Hookey Walker!' expressed incredulity

---

Chapter 28: A good-humoured Christmas Chapter, containing an Account of a Wedding, and some other Sports beside: which although in their way, even as good Customs as Marriage itself, are not quite so religiously kept up, in these degenerate Times

---

Pickwick, Sam and the Pickwickians travel down to Dingley Dell by coach. When they meet Wardle and his daughters, together with some young ladies who are down for the wedding, Snodgrass again devotes his attention to Miss Emily Wardle, while Winkle flirts with the black-eyed Miss Arabella Allen. That evening they enjoy Wardle's usual good hospitality, with whist and merriment. Next day, Mr Trundle and Bella Wardle are married. The wedding 'breakfast', at which Pickwick proposes the toast, is followed by a long walk, a dinner, and a ball. The following day is Christmas Eve, when the company kiss under the mistletoe, play traditional games, and pass the rest of the evening singing and listening to a story which is to be told by Wardle in the next chapter.

NOTES AND GLOSSARY:

new patent cabs:	Joseph A. Hansom patented the famous cab for two passengers in 1834
poussette:	a movement in a country dance, in which a couple circles with joined hands
snap-dragon:	Christmas game in which raisins are picked out of a bowl of burning brandy and eaten while still alight
wassail:	communal drink, especially spiced ale, for festive occasions

Chapter 29: The Story of the Goblins who stole a Sexton

Wardle tells a seasonal tale with an appropriate moral. One Christmas Eve, long ago, a mean-spirited sexton called Gabriel Grub goes to the churchyard at night to finish digging a grave. This gives him a grim sort of pleasure, as he can avoid his neighbours and the children of the town as they make merry together. When he has finished the grave, he is visited by goblins who convey him to their cavernous world under the earth. Here the sexton is soundly kicked, and is shown the error of his ways through a series of moving scenes in which humble people live in happiness, contentment and peace. Next morning, he wakes up in the churchyard and decides to leave the town. He returns years later, a poor but penitent and contented old man.

NOTES AND GLOSSARY:

gall and wormwood: 'Remembering mine affliction and my misery, the wormwood and the gall' (see the Bible, Lamentations 3:19)

Chapter 30: How the Pickwickians made and cultivated the Acquaintance of a couple of nice Young Men belonging to one of the Liberal Professions; how they disported themselves on the Ice; and how their first Visit came to a conclusion

On Christmas morning, Ben Allen, brother of the black-eyed Arabella, and his fellow medical student, Bob Sawyer, join the company at

Manor Farm. The jealous Winkle sees Bob as a potential rival for the affections of Arabella. When the party goes skating, Winkle again proves to be incompetent as a 'sportsman', and is called an impostor by Pickwick. Pickwick himself falls through the ice while sliding. He runs back to the house and goes to bed, where he drinks large quantities of hot punch with the male company and makes a complete recovery. The following day, when the visitors disperse to their homes, Pickwick is invited to meet some of Bob Sawyer's medical friends in London. He accepts the invitation with pleasure.

NOTES AND GLOSSARY:

barnacles:	(*colloquial*) spectacles
Cubas:	cigars made of Cuban tobacco
Guy's:	Guy's Hospital, London, founded by Thomas Guy in 1721

Chapter 31: Which is all about the Law, and sundry Great Authorities learned therein

Jackson, the clerk to Mrs Bardell's lawyers, Dodson and Fogg, issues subpoenas (see below) to the Pickwickians and Sam at Pickwick's temporary London lodgings at the George and Vulture. Next day, Pickwick consults his own lawyer, Perker, and is introduced to the haughty Serjeant Snubbin and the timid Mr Phunky, who are to defend him in court.

NOTES AND GLOSSARY:

half-price to the Adelphi Theatre: in Dickens's time, when part of a show was over, admission to a theatre was often at half-price

subpoena: (*Latin*) writ commanding a person to attend court. The shilling given to that person was a token payment towards his expenses

the settens after Term: the sittings in Hilary term, which begins in January

the secrets of the prison-house: 'I am forbid/To tell the secrets of my prison-house' (spoken by the Ghost in Shakespeare's *Hamlet*, 1.5.13–14)

Walentine's day: St Valentine's Day, 14 February, on which birds were supposed to pair, and young people traditionally choose their sweethearts

burked: William Burke was executed in 1829 for murdering people and selling their bodies for dissection

Serjeant Snubbin: see note on 'Afternoon' (p.26)

Chapter 32: Describes, far more fully than the Court Newsman ever did, a Bachelor's Party, given by Mr Bob Sawyer at his Lodgings in the Borough

Pickwick and his three friends spend the evening at Bob Sawyer's small and dingy lodgings. They listen to the stories of Bob's medical student friends and play cards with them. Mrs Raddle, Bob's landlady, is owed rent. She makes both Bob and his guests uncomfortable during the evening, and finally insists that all the guests leave the house when she hears them singing in the small hours.

NOTES AND GLOSSARY:

quarter-day:	rents were generally paid on the four quarter-days of the year
pattens:	built-up overshoes which protected footwear from mud and water
Bartholomew's:	St Bartholomew's Hospital
scorbutic:	like a person suffering from scurvy (a deficiency disease caused by lack of vitamin C)
anchors . . . emblems of hope:	'Which hope we have as an anchor of the soul' (see the Bible, Hebrews 6:19)
'natural':	when the dealer wins the trick because he has dealt himself twenty-one

Chapter 33: Mr Weller the elder delivers some Critical Sentiments respecting Literary Composition; and, assisted by his son Samuel, pays a small Instalment of Retaliation to the Account of the Reverend Gentleman with the Red Nose

Sam spends part of the day before Pickwick's trial carrying messages between his master and Perker. He then walks to Leadenhall Market, where he reads his father a 'valentine' he has written to Mary, the house-maid at Mayor Nupkins's house in Ipswich. He signs the valentine 'Pickwick'. Tony tells Sam of his plan to have the red-nosed, deputy shepherd, Stiggins, exposed at a temperance meeting. Father and son attend this meeting in Brick Lane, which is presided over by Mr Anthony Humm. Stiggins arrives fighting drunk and the meeting breaks up in confusion.

NOTES AND GLOSSARY:

cads:	omnibus conductors
cerulean:	deep blue
Prooshan Blue:	Prussian Blue, a dark blue. Sam refers to his father's complexion

valked out of a Sunday: probably refers to the fact that the law courts were closed on Sundays

profeel macheen: popular device which produced profile portraits

turpentine and bees'-vax: a mixture of turpentine and beeswax was used to polish furniture

the late Mr Dibdin: the song-writer Charles Dibdin (1745–1814)

Chapter 34: Is wholly devoted to a full and faithful Report of the memorable Trial of Bardell against Pickwick

---

The following day, Perker accompanies Pickwick and his friends to the court. The judge in the case is the short, fat and irritable Mr Justice Stareleigh, who falls asleep during the trial and contributes little of value. Mrs Bardell arrives with her friends, Mrs Cluppins and Mrs Sanders, and her young son, who is there to attract the sympathy of the judge and jury. Mrs Bardell's counsel, the red-faced Serjeant Buzfuz, opens the case for the plaintiff with a speech which distorts Pickwick's past acts and words, and especially two innocent and mundane notes which he sent to Mrs Bardell in her capacity as his landlady. After Mrs Cluppins has given evidence, Winkle enters the witness-box, and, harassed by Buzfuz's junior, Mr Skimpin, foolishly mentions Pickwick's innocent encounter with the lady in curlers at the Great White Horse inn, Ipswich. Tupman and Snodgrass have no choice but to confirm Winkle's testimony. In spite of Sam's success in making Buzfuz look foolish and Dodson and Fogg disreputable, and although Serjeant Snubbin tries to defend Pickwick's character, the case is lost, and Pickwick is ordered to pay £750 damages. On his way out of court, Pickwick informs Dodson and Fogg that he would rather spend his life in a debtors' prison than pay one farthing of costs or damages.

NOTES AND GLOSSARY:

the blue bag: barristers and solicitors traditionally carry blue bags, whereas more senior lawyers carry crimson ones

the students' box: section of the court which was reserved for law students

prayed a _tales_: asked that the jury be completed with _tales de circumstantibus_ (_Latin_), such persons from those standing about

Noakes, or Stoakes, or Stiles: fictitious names used in drafts of legal documents

Garraway's: a famous London coffee-house

tip-cheese: tip-cat, a game in which a small piece of wood is hit as far as possible with a stick

Chapter 35: In which Mr Pickwick thinks he had better go to Bath; and goes accordingly

Perker informs Pickwick that he has two months before Dodson and Fogg can have him arrested for non-payment of the costs and damages. Pickwick decides that he and his friends will go to Bath, as none of them has been there before. They travel to the west country with a fierce ex-army man, Mr Dowler, and his charming wife. Next morning, Dowler introduces Pickwick to his friend, the snobbish, dandified Master of Ceremonies of Bath, Angelo Cyrus Bantam, Esquire. Sam Weller gains some insight into Bath society when he meets Bantam's grandly dressed footman. That evening, Bantam presides over the dancing, tea-drinking, and card-playing at the famous Assembly Rooms. Pickwick is unimpressed by the foppish young men he meets, and is severely criticised for his mistakes at cards when he plays with the Dowager Lady Snuphanuph, Mrs Colonel Wugsby and Miss Bolo.

NOTES AND GLOSSARY:

a pewter half-crown: a counterfeit coin

'Moses': an actual coach-owner on the London to Bath run

this morning at two o'clock: in fashionable circles, 'morning' was the time before dinner rather than simply before noon

rappee: a coarse kind of snuff

girandoles: branched brackets or supports for candles

Chapter 36: The chief features of which, will be found to be an authentic Version of the Legend of Prince Bladud, and a most extraordinary Calamity that befel Mr Winkle

The Pickwickians share their lodgings in Bath with Mr and Mrs Dowler, and Pickwick himself settles down to a regular daily routine. One night, he discovers a manuscript which contains two versions of an old legendary account of the foundation of Bath by Bladud, the son of King Lud Hudibras. In the second of these the prince is disappointed in love, and is swallowed up by the earth at the spot where he prays that his hot tears may well up for ever. Since that time, according to the legend, people disappointed in their search for a marriage partner have visited the hot springs at that spot, in Bath. Having read the manuscript, Pickwick goes to bed. Dowler, who is meant to be waiting up for his wife, falls asleep. When Winkle opens the door at three o'clock in the morning it blows shut, leaving him on the pavement in his dressing-gown. Mrs Craddock, the landlady, sees him taking shelter in Mrs Dowler's sedan-chair, and assumes he is eloping with her. Mr Dowler chases Winkle round the Crescent. Winkle then barricades himself into his bedroom.

NOTES AND GLOSSARY:
Nash: the famous 'Beau Nash' became Master of Ceremonies in 1704
a deserving charity: here, the Bath Hospital
Pliny: Pliny the Elder, a Roman writer who tried to climb Vesuvius during an eruption, but was suffocated by volcanic fumes
Lud Hudibras: for the legend of King Hudibras, or Huddibras, and his son, Bladud, see Edmund Spenser's (1552?-99) *Faerie Queene*, II.10.25-6
King Cole: this nursery-rhyme figure was Coël, another legendary king of Britain
the arms o' Porpus: Morpheus, god of sleep in classical legend

---

Chapter 37: Honourably accounts for Mr Weller's Absence, by describing a Soirée to which he was invited and went; also relates how he was entrusted by Mr Pickwick with a Private Mission of Delicacy and Importance

---

Meanwhile, on the same day, Sam is invited to join a group of Bath footmen for one of their regular evenings together. John Smauker, Bantam's footman, escorts his guest to the back parlour of a local greengrocer, where a meal is to be served. The footmen are a proud and dignified group, but they like Sam, as do all members of the servant class. In the morning, Sam learns that Winkle has left for Bristol, and is sent in pursuit of him by Pickwick.

NOTES AND GLOSSARY:
airy bell: area bell, used for the servants' quarters 'below stairs'
killibeate: chalybeate, of water containing iron deposits
foil: thin material
kiver: shallow wooden vessel
srub: shrub, a mixture of fruit-juice and spirits

Chapter 38: How Mr Winkle, when he stepped out of the Frying-pan, walked gently and comfortably into the Fire

---

Having taken a room at the Bush inn, Bristol, Winkle sets out for Clifton and happens to ask the way at a doctor's surgery run by the now qualified Bob Sawyer and his friend Ben Allen. Ben tells Winkle that his sister, Arabella, seems not to like Bob Sawyer, as she has some prior attachment, and that she is living with an old aunt at present. When he returns to the inn, Winkle finds Dowler there and is surprised to discover that the apparently fearless man has in fact assumed that Winkle was planning a duel in Bath, and, like Winkle himself, has escaped to Bristol. Sam arrives at the Bush inn after midnight, and, after some discussion, agrees to stay and help Winkle find Arabella, if Pickwick gives his permission.

NOTES AND GLOSSARY:

flying the garter:	playing at a kind of leap-frog
jorum:	large drinking-bowl or its contents, especially punch
pennywinkle:	periwinkle, an edible mollusc
fanteegs:	states of anxiety or excitement

Chapter 39: Mr Samuel Weller, being entrusted with a Mission of Love, proceeds to execute it; with what success will hereinafter appear

Pickwick himself arrives in Bristol to make sure that Winkle's intentions are honourable. Sam is then sent to find out where Arabella is staying. By a stroke of good fortune he meets Mary, Nupkins's former housemaid, who is now working in a house near Clifton. She tells him that Arabella happens to be staying next door! Sam secretly arranges with Arabella that Winkle will see her the following evening. The tryst is duly accomplished with the help of Pickwick, in benevolent mood, and Sam, who gently hits a neighbouring 'scientific gentleman' on the head when he investigates the source of the light from Pickwick's lantern.

NOTES AND GLOSSARY:

Lor do adun:	Lord, do have done
the wandering Jew:	according to legend a Jew, called Ahasuerus in the best known version, scoffed at Christ as he carried the cross. He was condemned to wander about the world until the Second Coming
a dark lantern:	lantern with a shutter to reduce the light

Chapter 40: Introduces Mr Pickwick to a new and not uninteresting Scene in the great Drama of Life

The Pickwickians return to London for the new law term. Mr Namby, the Sheriff's Officer, arrives at the George and Vulture to arrest Pickwick, and has his hat knocked off by Sam. Namby's assistant, Smouch, accompanies Pickwick and Sam to the Officer's house. Perker again fails to persuade Pickwick to pay the legal costs and damages. Pickwick and Sam then go to the Fleet, a debtors' prison, by way of Serjeants' Inn.

NOTES AND GLOSSARY:

gig . . . guillotined cabriolet: all these one-horse vehicles have two wheels and no hood, hence they were known as 'guillotined'

Botany Bay: a penal settlement in New South Wales, Australia, to which convicts were transported in Dickens's time

Whitecross Street: debtors' prison

the ca-sa: writ of *capias ad satisfaciendum* (*Latin*), by which you may imprison the defendant until the plaintiff's claim is satisfied

habeas corpus: (*Latin*), a writ requiring that somebody be produced in person in court

tipstaff: court official

Chapter 41: What befel Mr Pickwick when he got into the Fleet; what Prisoners he saw there; and how he passed the Night

Pickwick is shown around the prison and observes that the debtors display a variety of responses to their circumstances. Sam considers that such imprisonment does not damage those who spend their time idling in public houses, but that it does damage honest working men. Before leaving for the night, Sam tells Pickwick the story of Number Twenty, a trusted long-stay prisoner who became frightened of the idea of being locked *out* of prison. Deeply disturbed by all that he has seen and heard, Pickwick falls asleep in the so-called warden's room, only to be woken up half an hour later by the other prisoners who sleep there. Mivins, 'The Zephyr', takes Pickwick's nightcap as a joke, and is punched by Pickwick. The prisoners respect Pickwick for this, and the newcomer agrees to pay for drinks. Smangle, a tall prisoner with bushy whiskers, tells so many stories that the others fall asleep while he is still talking.

NOTES AND GLOSSARY:

chevaux-de-frise: (*French*) spikes

the racket-ground: the ball game of rackets, or racquets, a game for two or four people, is played in a court enclosed with four high walls

all-fours: a card game for two players in which the players can score in four different ways: high, low, Jack, and the game

Zephyr . . . bears his name: that is, the wind

Court for the Relief of—: Insolvent Debtors. Imprisoned debtors applied to this court for release

Chapter 42: Illustrative, like the preceding one, of the old Proverb, that Adversity brings a Man acquainted with strange Bed-fellows. Likewise containing Mr Pickwick's extraordinary and startling announcement to Mr Samuel Weller

Sam returns next morning, and is not impressed by Smangle's manner and behaviour. Roker, the turnkey, at first arranges for Pickwick to share a room with a drunken chaplain, a violent butcher and a swindler. Pickwick learns that he can rent a single room from a pitifully thin 'Chancery prisoner' who has lived in the Fleet for twenty years, and Roker hires him furniture and various domestic items. Pickwick inspects the so-called 'poor side' of the prison, where he finds Jingle and Job Trotter in a destitute condition, and, moved by their suffering, gives them money. He tells Sam that the Fleet is no place for a young man, and that he must leave him, on full wages, during his imprisonment. This upsets Sam, who abruptly walks out. Although Pickwick calls after him, Sam does not return.

NOTES AND GLOSSARY:

a horse chaunter . . . a leg: a chaunter, or chanter, sells horses fraudulently; a leg is a swindler

Spout . . . uncle Tom: pawnbrokers (uncle Tom) had lifts (spouts) for carrying goods to storage rooms

Constable's Miscellany: a multi-volume miscellany of literature, the sciences and the arts (1826–35)

Chapter 43: Showing how Mr Samuel Weller got into Difficulties

In order to stay with Pickwick in the Fleet, Sam finds his father, at the Insolvent Court, and arranges that Tony will lend him twenty-five pounds and immediately have a writ issued against him for the debt. Mr Solomon Pell, an attorney who successfully defends one of Tony's fellow coachmen, accompanies Tony to the Temple, while Sam waits in a public house and sings a song. The company then take Pickwick's route to the Fleet, by way of Serjeants' Inn. Pickwick is astonished to see Sam return as a prisoner.

NOTES AND GLOSSARY:

'the Rules': area around certain prisons within which prisoners who put down money as security were allowed to live

a red-faced Nixon: the red-cheeked Robert Nixon figured in the frontispiece of popular editions of *Nixon's Prophecies*, first published in 1714

not generally known: the song is an adaptation of 'Turpin and the Bishop' in Horatio (Horace) Smith's (1779–1849) *Gaieties and Gravities* (1825)

prodigy son: for the parable of the prodigal son see the Bible, Luke 15

a ticket-porter: licensed messenger

Chapter 44: Treats of divers little Matters which occurred in the Fleet, and of Mr Winkle's mysterious Behaviour; and shows how the poor Chancery Prisoner obtained his Release at last

---

Sam tells Pickwick the remarkable story of a clerk who shot himself on principle. Sam soon settles to prison life, renting a small room from a bald-headed cobbler who has been in the Fleet since he became the innocent victim of a legal tangle over a will from which he was meant to benefit, twelve years ago. Smangle announces the arrival of Pickwick's three friends. The Pickwickians enjoy a hearty meal together, although Winkle is in a highly nervous condition. The consumptive Chancery prisoner dies after years of suffering.

NOTES AND GLOSSARY:

hare-skins: furs of hares and rabbits were worn next to the skin

Avay vith melincholly: lyric to a melody from Wolfgang Amadeus Mozart's (1756–91) opera *The Magic Flute* (1791)

Chapter 45: Descriptive of an Affecting Interview between Mr Samuel Weller and a Family Party. Mr Pickwick makes a Tour of the diminutive World he inhabits, and resolves to mix with it, in future, as little as possible

---

A few days later, Sam is visited by his father, together with his mother-in-law and the red-nosed Mr Stiggins, who are not aware of the secret arrangement between Sam and Tony. Mrs Weller and Stiggins are as hypocritical as ever, groaning over Sam's downfall but drinking what they are offered. When they have gone, Sam proves to be as charitable in his own way towards Job Trotter as Pickwick was to Jingle. All four men tour the prison, whose inmates lounge around in a noisy, chaotic environment. They drink gin which is smuggled in with the corrupt turnkeys' connivance. Although disturbed by what he sees and in failing health, Pickwick simply decides to stay in his room in future, and still refuses to pay his debts and thus get out of prison.

NOTES AND GLOSSARY:

picter-card: Sam refers to the fat King, one of the court-cards (or picture-cards)

Saint Simon Without, and Saint Walker Within: Without and Within
refer to parishes being outside or inside the City
boundaries. Tony comments on the discrepancy
between appearance and reality here, as the apostle
Simon's surname meant 'zealot', and 'Walker', also
used by Tony in Chapter 27, suggests that Stiggins
is an impostor

write a book about the 'Merrikins: Frances Trollope (1780–1863) made
money from her highly successful *Domestic Manners of the Americans* (1832)

Chapter 46: Records a touching Act of delicate Feeling, not unmixed with Pleasantry, achieved and performed by Messrs Dodson and Fogg

---

Mrs Bardell visits the Spaniards tea-gardens at Hampstead, accompanied by her son, Tommy, her lodger, Mrs Rogers, her friends, Mrs Sanders and Mrs Cluppins, the latter's sister, the domineering Mrs Raddle (Bob Sawyer's ex-landlady), and Mr Raddle, who can do nothing right in his wife's eyes. Jackson the clerk arrives to tell her that Dodson and Fogg require her urgently in the City. Without warning her, he takes her straight to the Fleet, together with Tommy and her two friends. This is because, after the Pickwick trial, Dodson and Fogg tricked her into signing a legal document which made her liable for the amount of her costs. When Sam sees her in the Fleet, he realises that some good may come of her imprisonment, and sends Job Trotter hurrying off to Perker's office.

NOTES AND GLOSSARY:

cognovit: (*Latin*) 'An acknowledgement by a defendant that the plaintiff's cause is just; in which case the defendant, to save expense, suffers judgement to be entered against him without trial' (Oxford English Dictionary)

Chapter 47: Is chiefly devoted to matters of Business, and the temporal Advantage of Dodson and Fogg. Mr Winkle re-appears under extraordinary circumstances. Mr Pickwick's Benevolence proves stronger than his Obstinacy

---

Job Trotter gives Sam's message to Perker at his house that evening, with the help of Lowten. Next morning, Perker explains to Pickwick that Mrs Bardell's future is in his hands. Perker has already seen her. She agreed to forgo the legal damages and to write a letter denouncing Dodson and Fogg if Pickwick would pay her costs as well as his own, thus freeing them both. Before Pickwick can reply, Winkle arrives with Arabella. They eloped with the help of Mary the house-maid and were married three days ago. It appears that Perker has encouraged Winkle to implore Pickwick to speak to Bob Allen on his behalf, which Pickwick can do only if he leaves the Fleet. When Tup-man and Snodgrass arrive, all the arguments are gone over again, leav-ing Pickwick defenceless against the pleas of his friends. As Sam and Pickwick leave the Fleet, they show their usual generosity towards their fellow prisoners. Pickwick arranges for Perker to return to the prison the following day to talk with Jingle.

NOTES AND GLOSSARY:
the law of demises: law concerning the transfer of estates by will or by lease

---

Chapter 48: Relates how Mr Pickwick, with the Assistance of Samuel Weller, essayed to soften the heart of Mr Benjamin Allen, and to mollify the wrath of Mr Robert Sawyer

---

Arabella's old aunt is driven to Bob Sawyer's surgery by Martin, the surly groom, where she announces that Arabella has run away and got married. Ben Allen is so upset that he attacks Martin and is promptly knocked down. Pickwick and Sam arrive to find the place in confusion. Ben, his aunt and Bob Sawyer are at first furious with them for appar-ently encouraging the elopement, but Pickwick's wise words have a soothing effect, and eventually they all part as friends. Pickwick and Sam return to the Bush inn, where they settle down to listen to a story told by the one-eyed bagman, whose tale of Tom Smart in the Peacock at Eatanswill figured in Chapter 14.

NOTES AND GLOSSARY:
Camphor-julep: stimulant mixture of camphor and syrup
a bowl of bishop: sweet compound of wine, sugar and fruits, especially mulled, spiced port

---

Chapter 49: Containing the Story of the Bagman's Uncle

The bagman's uncle, Jack Martin, a friend of Tom Smart, was a jolly, energetic man, whose business used to take him to Scotland. One night, according to Martin, he has supper with an Edinburgh family and sets off for his lodgings on foot in the small hours. Seeing a collection of old mail coaches, all of which have fallen into decay, he sits down and dozes off. At two o'clock he wakes up to find that the coaches are in working order and surrounded by groups of people in eighteenth-century costume. He boards the Edinburgh-to-London coach, which he shares with a beautiful woman who is being abducted by the son of the Marquess of Filletoville, whom she will be forced to marry. She and Martin later manage to kill this young man and the brute who accompanies him. Martin vows that he will never marry another woman. Having woken up in the grey light of morning to find that the coaches are again empty shells, he is true to his word, and remains a bachelor for the rest of his life.

NOTES AND GLOSSARY:
a Baillie: Scottish municipal magistrate
"Willie brewed a peck o' maut": a song by Robert Burns (1759–96)
Arthur's Seat: a hill overlooking Edinburgh
Newport market: London meat market
in the cockchafer fashion: like large beetles pinned up for display
breaks: large wagonettes

Chapter 50: How Mr Pickwick sped upon his Mission, and how he was reinforced in the Outset by a most unexpected Auxiliary

---

Pickwick and Sam travel from Bristol to Birmingham with Ben Allen in order to see Winkle's father and explain matters to him. Bob Sawyer also goes with them, and performs various antics on top of the coach. By the time they reach Birmingham, Bob and Ben are feeling the effects of the day's drinking. When they accompany Pickwick to the house of Mr Winkle senior, a businessman, they make the interview even more difficult than it might have been. Mr Winkle reads a letter from his son explaining about his marriage to Arabella, and angers Pickwick by coolly saying that he refuses to have anything more to do with young Winkle.

NOTES AND GLOSSARY:
wharfinger: wharf-owner
Mr Grimaldi: Joseph Grimaldi (1779–1837), a famous clown. Dickens edited his *Memoirs* in 1838

Chapter 51: In which Mr Pickwick encounters an old Acquaintance. To which fortunate circumstance the Reader is mainly indebted for matter of thrilling interest herein set down, concerning two great Public Men of might and power

---

The four travellers set off for London, but stop for the night at the Saracen's Head, Towcester, because of the heavy rain. Mr Pott, editor of the 'Blue' Eatanswill Gazette, is at the same inn, and joins them for dinner. Mr Slurk, Pott's rival at the 'Buff' Eatanswill Independent, arrives later in the evening. Pickwick and Sam have to separate the newspaper men when they start a brawl in the kitchen. Next morning, in better weather, Pickwick and his companions continue on their way to London.

NOTES AND GLOSSARY:

an additional duty: extra window tax

the Humane Society: society for the rescue of drowning people

'Wotever is, is right': the last words in Pope's *Essay on Man*, Epistle I (1733)

a dead donkey: Sam refers to Laurence Sterne's (1713–68) *A Sentimental Journey through France and Italy* (1768), 'The Bidet' (that is, post-horse) and 'Nampont. The Dead Ass'

Lights in the Sun: public rooms in inns were often given names in Dickens's time

---

Chapter 52: Involving a serious Change in the Weller Family, and the untimely Downfall of the red-nosed Mr Stiggins

---

Mary the housemaid gives Sam a letter, dictated by his father, informing him that Mrs Weller has died of a cold caught when listening to a sermon in the rain. He goes down to Dorking, where Tony tells him that he is becoming a coachman again and selling the business, in order to avoid the numerous widows who fussed over him the moment his second wife died. Mr Stiggins comes into the Marquis of Granby to find out whether he figured in Mrs Weller's will. When he helps himself to his favourite rum, Tony literally kicks him out and gives him a ducking in a neighbouring horse-trough.

NOTES AND GLOSSARY:

a patent Brahmin: Joseph Bramah patented a safety-lock in 1784

four and a half per cent. reduced counsels: when Consols, that is Consolidated Annuities, were introduced, some government annuities of more than three per cent were combined and reduced to that standard figure

---

Chapter 53: Comprising the final Exit of Mr Jingle and Job Trotter; with a Great Morning of Business in Gray's Inn Square. Concluding with a Double Knock at Mr Perker's door

---

Arabella is distressed to hear that Winkle's father has threatened to withdraw his assistance, but is comforted by Pickwick, who hints that he would help the couple if necessary. Pickwick goes to Perker's to discuss his legal affairs. First Jingle and Job Trotter arrive. Pickwick has provided the money for their release and for their passage to the West Indies, where they will get work. When they have left, Dodson and Fogg come for their money. As they gloat over their success, Pickwick loses his temper and frightens them away. Yet another visitor announces himself by knocking hard on Perker's door.

Chapter 54: Containing some Particulars relative to the Double Knock, and other Matters: among which certain Interesting Disclosures relative to Mr Snodgrass and a Young Lady are by no means irrelevant to this History

Joe, the fat boy, has fallen asleep while knocking on the door. Old Wardle arrives. He announces that he has angrily refused Snodgrass permission to marry his daughter, Emily. Joe discovers the lovers embracing at Wardle's hotel, but is bribed by them and given a meal by Mary in order to keep their secret. Snodgrass hides in Wardle's bedroom when the latter returns to the hotel with Pickwick, Winkle, and Ben Allen. During dinner, the embarrassed Snodgrass comes out of the bedroom. Wardle is angry at first, but soon relents. Perker joins the company for a happy evening.

NOTES AND GLOSSARY:
charcoal:	refers to suicide by inhaling the fumes from a charcoal fire

Chapter 55: Mr Solomon Pell, assisted by a Select Committee of Coachmen, arranges the Affairs of the elder Mr Weller

Sam explains to his father that he has to get probate of his wife's will. Sam and Tony,. together with three of the latter's coachmen friends, go to see Mr Pell the attorney, who sees the will through the inevitable legal complexities. Pell then puts the sale and transferring of the stock in the hands of Wilkins Flasher, a stockbroker who makes private bets with the equally 'flashy' Mr Simmery. Tony gets his money and heads for the George and Vulture with Sam.

NOTES AND GLOSSARY:
Abernethy biscuit:	hard biscuit flavoured with caraway-seeds
in Queer Street:	people in trouble, especially of a financial kind, are said to be in this imaginary street
inexpressibles:	euphemism for breeches or trousers
P.P.:	play or pay

Chapter 56: An important Conference takes place between Mr Pickwick and Samuel Weller, at which his Parent assists. An old Gentleman in a snuff-coloured Suit arrives unexpectedly

Sam and Tony have some difficulty in persuading Pickwick to look after Tony's money, but eventually they succeed. Pickwick privately informs Tony about Sam and Mary. He then tells Sam that he would like to set the couple up in some kind of small business or situation. Sam strongly expresses his loyalty to Pickwick, however, and says that Mary is willing to wait for him. Mr Winkle's father arrives from Birmingham and walks into Arabella's room without revealing his identity. He tells her how hurtful it is when children get married without asking their parents' permission. When Winkle returns and his father's identity is revealed, the old man forgives the couple and makes friends with Pickwick.

Chapter 57: In which the Pickwick Club is finally dissolved, and everything concluded to the satisfaction of everybody

After a week of secret business, Pickwick tells the company at a dinner held by Wardle that he has taken and furnished a house at Dulwich, near London, and that Snodgrass and Emily Wardle are to be married from the house. He also announces the dissolution of the Pickwick Club. After four hectic days of preparation, many characters gather at Dulwich for the wedding, after which the company enjoys a happy wedding breakfast in Pickwick's new home. Dickens, as author, takes his leave of his characters, and briefly outlines their subsequent lives. Sam sticks to his word and remains Pickwick's faithful servant for two years. After this time, Pickwick's old housekeeper dies. Mary takes her place and is married to Sam. He and Pickwick always remain very closely attached to one another.

NOTES AND GLOSSARY:
passed through the Gazette: been declared bankrupt

Part 3

Commentary

Structure and plot

Serialisation

By the spring of 1837, monthly numbers of *Pickwick* had been appearing in their familiar blue-green paper covers for a year, and sales were running at more than twenty thousand copies a month, a figure which was almost doubled by the time publication ended in November. Yet the first few numbers sold in hundreds rather than thousands, and failed completely in the provinces. How did Dickens manage to make such a great success of a project which had a very unpromising beginning?

The story of Dickens's agreement to write a book which was to be 'illustrative of manners and life in the Country', and of his subsequent control over the direction the novel was actually to take, after the death of the first illustrator, Seymour, is a complex one.* Once he had taken full charge of the project, and had Hablot Browne (whose pseudonym was 'Phiz') as his illustrator, Dickens proved to be a natural and brilliant improviser. The first few numbers (see Part 2) contained a series of improvised set pieces of amusing, but unconnected and often trivial action. When Sam Weller was introduced in the fourth number, sales rose, and Dickens developed this improvised character in subsequent numbers.

In June 1836, Dickens reported the Norton-Melbourne adultery case for the *Morning Chronicle*, and in the following month wrote the chapter in which Mrs Bardell faints in Pickwick's arms. He clearly wrote this scene with a view to developing the Bardell-Pickwick case in later numbers. At this point, therefore, we see Dickens planning ahead rather than simply improvising a number of unconnected incidents. Significantly, the Bardell-Pickwick case was also used as the main springboard for his satiric attack on the English legal system. Re-read the general summary in Part 2, and consider how the content of the monthly numbers becomes increasingly unified as the novel unfolds, although Dickens's comic improvisation of local detail is sustained throughout. Notice, for example, how his attack on the law is first aimed at a number of lawyers and a magistrate, and is later more fully developed in the trial and the

*See Patten's introduction to the Penguin edition, Penguin Books, Harmondsworth, 1972, for a detailed account of the remarkable publishing history of *Pickwick*.

portrayal of the Fleet prison. As the novel centres increasingly on the activities of Pickwick and Sam, Pickwick's three friends, and especially Tupman and Snodgrass, become far less significant characters than they were in the first few numbers. Writing the novel month by month allowed Dickens to change the direction of the plot as he went along. To what extent do you consider the overall structure of the novel to be loose as a result?

Butt and Tillotson have pointed out that the duration of the action of the novel matches the nineteen months of serial publication, and that the action of each monthly number is set in the same month, or thereabouts, nine years earlier than the years of publication.* Christmas at Dingley Dell is described in the January number, for example, and the final (double) number opens on an October morning. Dickens organised the time scheme of the novel in such a way that in any particular month his readers would be wondering what Pickwick and Sam were doing, and could then satisfy their curiosity by reading the next number. In what other ways would Dickens's organisation of his material in monthly numbers have kept up his readers' interest in the novel's characters and themes?

Characterisation in *Pickwick* is also affected by this serial method of publication, as Dickens emphasised idiosyncratic features of his characters partly in order to help his readers to identify them, often after an absence from the plot of several months. Consider, for example, how Jingle's extraordinary *staccato* style of speech immediately identifies him at each new encounter, even before Pickwick has seen him or heard his name mentioned (see, for instance, Chapters 7 and 15).

Before embarking on *Pickwick*, Dickens's literary friends had advised him not to write a serial novel, as they considered this to be a 'low' form of publication. His friends proved to be wrong, for he triumphantly revitalised the serial publication of fiction, and thus inaugurated an era of serial novel-writing which produced not only his own greatest novels but also those of Thackeray, Trollope, and George Eliot, among other major Victorian novelists.

A novel and a miscellany

Butt and Tillotson suggest that 'a quarter of the way through its course, *Pickwick* discovers its shape, with the emergence of Sam and the beginning of the action of Bardell v. Pickwick', but add that 'as it grew into a novel, *Pickwick* did not lose its character as a miscellany, with a "free range of English scenes and people", nor its loosely picaresque form'.†

*John Butt and Kathleen Tillotson, *Dickens at Work*, Methuen, London, 1957, p.73.
†*Dickens at Work*, pp.71–2.

These remarks sum up the main characteristics of the structure and plot of the novel.

The early chapters contain a number of comic adventures, in all of which the Pickwickians look foolish in one way or another, and describe various aspects of country life, such as shooting, riding and a game of cricket. As well as observing human nature in all its aspects, the Pickwickians listen to a variety of tales, told by a number of different characters. Thus 'miscellany' seems a fair description. Notice, moreover, that numerous comic incidents are also improvised in the middle and later chapters of the book. The loosely picaresque form allows considerable flexibility as the novel takes shape. Early on, a coaching tour allows the retired Pickwick to examine his fellow Englishmen at leisure, as well as to get into a number of comic predicaments, and to move from snug hearth to cosy inn, listening to dark tales which contrast with Pickwick's own view of the world. His travelling becomes more purposeful when he is in pursuit of Jingle, and thus closely engaged in the righting of a wrong. His last tour is a selfless mission on Winkle's behalf, which successfully repairs family ties which have been in danger of breaking. But although Pickwick's travels become less inconsequential as the plot takes shape, there is almost always enough slack in the loose structure of the novel to allow for minor comic incidents to be introduced.

Pickwick does not have a main plot until the Bardell-Pickwick case is developed, and then virtually everything in the novel is seen in relation to that. For example, Sam Weller's step-mother figures prominently in the Tony Weller sub-plot, and is the most important of several troublesome widows in the novel who reflect the difficulties Mrs Bardell poses Pickwick in the main plot. Although it would be possible to list a number of sub-plots which run through the novel as it unfolds, such as Winkle's courtship and marriage and Jingle's adventures and eventual imprisonment in the Fleet, clearly the main sub-plot is that of Sam Weller's 'below stairs' life with his fellow servants and his father, Tony. This sub-plot complements the main plot in the sense that Pickwick's 'above stairs' encounters with a range of people and problems (Jingle, Mayor Nupkins, the haughty upper classes at Bath) are paralleled in Sam's life as Pickwick's servant (Job Trotter, Grummer, and the Bath footmen). So important does Sam become in the novel, however, that any claim that he represents 'low life', or merely offers comic relief during the episodes in the Fleet, can be dismissed as absurd. Indeed, his function is in one sense pivotal, in that Dickens explores the theme of parenthood and familial love by making him become, as it were, the surrogate son of Pickwick, while remaining the dutiful son of his true father, Tony.

The Fleet chapters of *Pickwick* draw the main plot and the various sub-plots together, for not only are Pickwick and Sam, Jingle and Job Trotter, and finally Mrs Bardell actually imprisoned there, but Tony Weller, Mrs Weller and Stiggins visit Sam, the Pickwickians visit Pickwick, and, after Mrs Bardell's arrest, Winkle arrives with his new bride. After Pickwick's release, all the entangled threads are unravelled, and the wedding in Dulwich in the last chapter marks the departure of the characters into the future, which Dickens briefly sketches.

One of the weaknesses of the overall loosely picaresque form of *Pickwick*, however, is the limitation it imposes on the development of all but a few central relationships. Most of the huge number of minor characters in the novel are encountered briefly, and are then, so to speak, left behind as the coach rattles on. On the other hand, as Dickens does not set out to create psychologically complex characters in the novel, the reader is less disturbed than usual by the licence he takes with certain 'realistic' conventions, such as coincidence. For example, Mary, Nupkins's housemaid, happens to change employer in Ipswich, and then that employer happens to move to a house next door to Arabella Allen's aunt in Clifton (Chapter 39). Moreover, Winkle happens to ask the way to Clifton at Bob Sawyer's surgery in Bristol (Chapter 38). Dickens indicates to the reader that he is manipulating the plot by openly referring to the 'accident', for example, which 'threw' Mary in Sam's way (Chapter 39).

This is one way in which Dickens loosens the constraints of more strictly 'realistic' fiction in the novel. Similarly, Pickwick is a man of means who never wants for money, and this gives him great freedom of action. What other kinds of freedom from normal constraints are evident in *Pickwick*?

Style and narrative technique

Dickens's comic style

The great interest which *Pickwick* generated in England as it was published in monthly numbers is reflected in Elizabeth Gaskell's (1810–65) famous novel *Cranford* (first book edition 1853), when Captain Brown is run down by a train, partly as the result of his being engrossed in the latest number. In the first chapter of *Cranford*, the Captain praises young 'Boz', but is sharply told by the conservative Miss Jenkyns that no new writer could possibly approach that eighteenth-century literary giant, Dr Johnson (1709–84). This is a significant difference of opinion, for behind it lies a clue to Dickens's impact as a highly original novelist in the 1830s and 1840s. Whereas Dr Johnson's style is balanced, learned and grand, Dickens's is often boisterously impressionistic, exaggerated and flexible in its effects. In *Pickwick*, these characteristics of Dickens's prose style reflect the liveliness of his comic invention of both action and character. Let us consider some of the ways in which style, action and character are related.

First, much of the comic action shows us that there is a wide gap between appearance and reality in the lives of the characters. For example, Winkle is an incompetent horseman, yet he is dressed as a 'sportsman', and is taken to be 'sporting', early in the novel. In Chapter 5, Dickens describes the mishaps on the road to Dingley Dell in a cool, precise, rather pedantic style which, being in a sense inappropriate in its understatement, makes the farcical events of the chapter seem even funnier than they would be if described in a style more obviously appropriate to farce. The precision of the style reflects the kind of control and orderliness with which the Pickwickians would like to be associated (appearance), whereas the events described indicate the real state of affairs. Consider this sentence: 'The horse no sooner beheld Mr Pickwick advancing towards him with the chaise whip in his hand, than he exchanged the rotatory motion in which he had previously indulged, for a retrograde movement of so very determined a character, that it at once drew Mr Winkle, who was still at the end of the bridle, at a rather quicker rate than fast walking, in the direction from which they had just come' (Chapter 5). The understated quality of the second half of this sentence ('that it at once drew . . .') is so much more telling than more obviously representative phrasing, such as 'sent Winkle flying', would have been.

Secondly, Dickens exploits his genius for mimicry in his characters' speech. The Wellers' cockney slang and confused v's and w's, Jingle's *staccato* style of speech, and Grummer's Suffolk accent, are a few examples. What others can you identify, and how does Pickwick's style of speech compare with these accents and unusual styles? Related to Dickens's use of these various individual styles of speech is his handling of the more generic styles of professions or groups, such as the parliamentary style of the meeting of the Pickwick Club: 'Mr BLOTTON (of Aldgate) rose to order. Did the honourable Pickwickian allude to him?', and so on (Chapter 1). Then there is the hyperbolic and heavily adjectival newspaper style of the Eatanswill Gazette: 'a scene of varied and delicious enchantment—a bewildering coruscation of beauty and talent—a lavish and prodigal display of hospitality . . .' (Chapter 15). Compare this with Serjeant Buzfuz's description of Mr Bardell's death (in fact having been knocked on the head with a quart pot in a public house cellar), in the pathetic style of the persuasive lawyer: 'glided almost imperceptibly from the world, to seek elsewhere for that repose and peace which a custom-house can never afford' (Chapter 34). (Notice again the gap between appearance and reality here.)

Thirdly, Dickens describes places and groups of people with an energy which characterises his writing from *Sketches by Boz* to *Edwin Drood*. Perhaps his favourite descriptive device is repetition, through which the impression he wishes to create is built up through a sentence or paragraph until the reader feels that every detail in the scene is part of a larger whole, and shares some dominant characteristic. For example, he creates the impression of a bustling crowd at the Eatanswill election by beginning five consecutive sentences in one paragraph with the words 'There was . . .' or 'There were . . .', and by using the same syntactic structure ('and the flags were rustling, and the band was playing . . .') in no less than seven consecutive clauses in the last sentence of the paragraph (Chapter 13).

The above are comparatively extreme examples of Dickens's remarkably flexible prose style, chosen to illustrate points about his style as sharply as possible. Much of Dickens's prose in *Pickwick* is, of course, comparatively 'quiet', and, in his detailed treatment of speech habits, clothes, houses, and so on, he suggests that, for all their oddities, his characters inhabit the world of commonplace reality which we too know.

Steven Marcus describes Dickens's style in *Pickwick* with admirable succinctness:

> It is a style which is perfectly dramatic and functional while at the same time announcing its imaginative autonomy, calling itself to our notice as poetry does, and with an unimpeded strength and ease, a deftness and speed and subtlety, entirely new to the novel of Dickens's day.*

The author as editor and narrator

In his 'Preface to the Original Edition' (1837), Dickens writes of himself, as 'author':

> Deferring to the judgment of others [that is, Seymour, and Chapman and Hall] in the outset of the undertaking, he adopted the machinery of the club, which was suggested as that best adapted to his purpose: but, finding that it tended rather to his embarrassment than otherwise, he gradually abandoned it, considering it a matter of very little importance to the work whether strictly epic justice were awarded to the club, or not.

We have seen that Dickens gained complete control over the 'undertaking' after the death of Seymour, his first illustrator. *Pickwick*'s three friends figure less prominently as the novel develops and the Club fades into the background. This gradual abandonment of the 'machinery of

*Steven Marcus, *Dickens: From Pickwick to Dombey*, Chatto and Windus, London, 1965, p.15.

the club' affects not only the content of the novel, but also its narrative technique.

In the first paragraph of the first chapter, Dickens describes himself as the 'editor' of the papers of the Pickwick Club. We gather that these papers include its official transactions and the notebooks of Pickwick and his friends, who form the Club's Corresponding Society. This convention of the author of a fictional work presenting himself as the editor of material written by others is an old one, but perhaps the most interesting and fully developed recent precedent was Carlyle's *Sartor Resartus* (1833–4), published in serial form only a few years before *Pickwick*. (*Sartor* was to influence Dickens's later, social novels.)

Dickens also refers to his 'editorial functions' in the opening paragraph of Chapter 4, and goes on to say that the particulars recorded in this and 'the succeeding chapter' are drawn from Snodgrass's notebook. This reliance upon one of the fictional characters for information is used for comic effect in the description of the celebrations after the cricket match, when Dickens, as editor, says that although Snodgrass took a great mass of notes, as usual, the 'influence of the wine' upon that gentleman made his hand so unsteady 'as to render his writing nearly unintelligible, and his style wholly so' (Chapter 7). Similarly, Dickens playfully withholds Pickwick's heart-rending description of the abandoned Miss Wardle from the reader, but refers to his notebook, 'blotted with the tears of sympathising humanity', which lies open before him (Chapter 10).

Although Dickens makes other references to Pickwick's describing his own actions, for example, this editorial narrative technique is never fully developed, and gradually disappears altogether. By the halfway point in *Pickwick*, Dickens has established a sufficiently strong identity as authorial narrator of the novel to be able to introduce his description of Christmas at Dingley Dell with a page of his own thoughts on the meaning of the great Christian festival: 'We write these words now, many miles distant from the spot at which, year after year, we met on that day, a merry and joyous circle . . .' (Chapter 28). Dickens also occasionally refers to his readers, as in the opening sentence of number XII: 'The morning of the thirteenth of February, which the readers of this authentic narrative know, as well as we do, to have been the day immediately preceding that which was appointed for the trial of Mrs Bardell's action, was a busy time for Mr Samuel Weller' (Chapter 33). This narrative *self-consciousness* is also evident in those chapter titles which draw attention to the organisation of the novel into chapters (for instance, Chapter 15) or even to the problem of writing chapter titles (Chapter 16). Henry Fielding addresses his readers in the last book of *Tom Jones* (1749) as fellow-travellers who have journeyed through the many pages of the novel with him. Although Dickens does not make his role as authorial narrator one of the subjects of *Pickwick*, as Fielding does in *Tom Jones*, we sense his guiding hand throughout the work, first as 'editor', but as author or creator throughout.

The interpolated tales

The nine so-called interpolated tales in *Pickwick* have not generally been regarded as particularly good stories in themselves. Moreover, critics of the novel have often assumed that they were merely pieces which Dickens had ready for publication in journals, and simply dropped into his novel whenever he was short of material. This last view has, however, been challenged in recent years, and particularly by Robert Patten.* Patten and others have shown that Dickens not only liked his tales, just as he always enjoyed blood-and-thunder melodrama, but that the tales were part of the artistic design of *Pickwick*, loose though that design undeniably is. Let us consider two ways in which the tales are related to the main narrative in the novel.

First, they often provide a *contrast* to the tone or atmosphere of the novel. Notice how several of the earlier tales, such as 'The Stroller's Tale' (Chapter 3), 'The Convict's Return' (Chapter 6), and 'A Madman's Manuscript' (Chapter 11), embody grim, dark views of the world which contrast starkly with the lightheartedness of Dickens's main narrative, in which he describes the ridiculous escapades of Pickwick and his friends. As the novel darkens, and the law and the Fleet prison cast their shadow over the novel, the stories lighten. (At least two of the lighter tales, those concerning Prince Bladud (Chapter 36) and the Bagman's uncle (Chapter 49), were certainly written by Dickens at the time he wrote the monthly numbers in which they figure.)

Secondly, some of the stories also *complement* the main narrative thematically. For example, Steven Marcus shows that the theme of fathers and sons, which Dickens develops in Sam's relationships with Tony, his real father, and Pickwick, his surrogate father, is also to be found in several of the interpolated tales,† although, again, the vindictiveness of some of these tales contrasts with the spirit of the novel itself. Similarly, the tale called 'A Madman's Manuscript', which concerns a madman whose wife married him for his money, follows the chapter in which Jingle, who wants to marry Miss Rachael Wardle for her money, is tracked down in London and paid off by Perker (Chapter 10). In a much lighter vein, the widow in 'The Bagman's Story' (Chapter 14) complements the numerous other widows in the novel.

Although it can certainly be argued that the interpolated tales are

---

*Robert L. Patten, 'The Art of *Pickwick*'s Interpolated Tales', *English Literary History*, 34, 1967, pp.349–66.
†Steven Marcus, *Dickens: From Pickwick to Dombey*, p.42.

part of the artistic design, the fact remains that the earlier, grimmer tales particularly stand out like black blots in the bright pages of the first quarter of the novel. We have seen that Dickens took some time to develop a main plot in the novel, and that the early chapters can fairly be described as a miscellany. The first few stories also seem to indicate that Dickens was deeply aware of the darker side of life, but could not accommodate it in the novel proper. He therefore introduced these starkly contrastive stories. He seems to have had a similar problem in *The Old Curiosity Shop*, published not long after *Pickwick*, in which the unrelieved goodness of Little Nell is kept separate from the evil Quilp, for most of the novel. This separation is perhaps the main weakness of that novel. To what extent do you consider the separation of good and evil in the early chapters of *Pickwick* to be a weakness?

Probably the most impressive of the interpolated tales is 'The Story of the Goblins who stole a Sexton' (Chapter 29), told by the affable Wardle on Christmas Eve at Manor Farm, Dingley Dell. This seasonal story anticipates Dickens's later Christmas Books, such as the famous *Christmas Carol* (1843), in several ways, but most obviously in the conversion of the mean-spirited sexton through his exposure to a number of domestic scenes which illustrate that humble people can live happily together in mutual love. The sexton's name, Gabriel Grub, suggests that he is, as it were, the larva (or grub) stage of an angel (Gabriel), who must change his present state in order to take flight. (It is perhaps significant that the Victorians often used the analogy of the larva when discussing Christian ideas concerning the resurrection of the dead.) Patten claims that this tale of conversion from mean-spiritedness to good-heartedness is central, both literally (being in the middle of the novel) and metaphorically in *Pickwick*, and that it 'stands as an epitome of the whole novel'.* The Dingley Dell context in which the tale is told is certainly important, for it underlines the 'Christmas spirit' moral of both the tale and the novel as a whole.

Characterisation

Varieties and shades of human character

Of all Dickens's remarkable gifts, it is perhaps his ability to create what appears to be a whole world of characters which has most consistently impressed successive generations of readers. Dickens himself claimed that his characters somehow 'appeared' before him as he worked on his novels, and that he simply set them down. In his first novel they certainly appeared in large numbers, for there are over one hundred

*Patten, 'The Art of *Pickwick*'s Interpolated Tales', *English Literary History*, 34, 1967, p.363.

characters in *Pickwick*. (See the Penguin edition for a list of the characters, with brief descriptions.) Many of these are encountered only
briefly by Pickwick on his travels, as he mixes 'with different varieties
and shades of human character' (Chapter 57). This proliferation of
minor characters, however, helps to give the impression of a bustling,
but none too saintly English nation going about its daily business as
the Pickwickians make their tours. Although we see more of life in
coaching inns and in lawyers' offices than in provincial houses or fac-
tories or working farms, we are introduced to a wide range of social
groups, from the numerous members of the servant class in the novel
to the high society of Bath, and from the lawyer's clerk to the leading
barrister and the judge. There are more lawyers (at least eight significant
minor characters) than there are members of any other profession.
These lawyers are worthy of attention not only in themselves, as individual characters (Buzfuz, Dodson and Fogg, Perker, Solomon Pell),
but also as a group, working in the dingy confines of legal chambers and
courts, and wielding considerable power over the destiny of the ordinary
men and women who get caught up in the machinery of the law.

Dickens was to develop a technique in his later novels whereby the
inner anxieties, drives and neuroses of his characters are reflected in the
outer world as they perceive or shape it, and in their physical appearance, dress, speech, mannerisms, and so on. As inner lives are related
to the outer world, the inanimate often appears to become animate, and
vice versa. Even as early as *Pickwick* we can see that Dickens often uses
a character's clothes, house or possessions to reflect his or her personality. Consider the arrival of Mr Namby, the sheriff's deputy, at the
George and Vulture, where he is to arrest Pickwick: 'Sam was taking
the air in George Yard, when a queer sort of fresh painted vehicle drove
up, out of which there jumped with great agility, throwing the reins to a
stout man who sat beside him, a queer sort of gentleman, who seemed
made for the vehicle, and the vehicle for him' (Chapter 40). The double
repetition of 'a queer sort of . . .' and 'made for the vehicle, and the
vehicle for him' implicitly encourages us to then examine the vehicle
to discover the man: 'It was painted a bright yellow, with the shafts and
wheels picked out in black'; the horse has 'something of a flash and
dog-fighting air about him', which accords 'both with the vehicle and
his master'. We then learn that Namby dresses 'in a particularly gor-
geous manner', wears very large pieces of jewellery, and uses a 'very
bright and glaring silk handkerchief'. The vehicle, the horse, the clothes,
the jewellery, the handkerchief, and the man are all of a piece, and the
flashy Namby's speech and actions confirm the impression of him which
Dickens has established in the first couple of paragraphs. Dozens of the
minor characters in the novel figure in only one small episode, but are,
as it were, caught and fixed by Dickens in some habitual act or pose

which vividly suggests the kind of people they are and the kind of life they lead. Our view of them is limited to what might be called their ruling passions, for they are not given space in which to develop, or even to show signs that they have more to them.

Although much more space is obviously devoted to the few major characters in the novel, they too *develop* very little, if at all. Even in his portrayal of Pickwick, Dickens's treatment of character is not psychological, in the sense that he does not explore the fine shadings of thought and feeling which register, for example, the complexities of contradictory motives, confused emotions, or undeveloped ideas. In the trial chapter, Dickens does not tell or show us what is going on in Pickwick's mind, with the result that his refusal to pay the costs and damages at the end of the chapter has considerable dramatic impact, but is seen by the reader as if from a distance (Chapter 34). Although Sam Weller's relationships with his father and with Pickwick are crucial, they can hardly be said to develop significantly. Indeed, our lack of a sense in *Pickwick* of a world in which people's relationships with each other are constantly changing and developing, even if only in small ways, can be tested by asking ourselves whether we imagine those people sustaining their relationships when we are reading an episode in which they do not figure. Dickens's comic vision in *Pickwick* tends both to distance and to isolate his characters, so that we are not drawn into the ebb and flow of their reactions to one another.

Samuel Pickwick

We learn very little about Pickwick's former life, but gather, almost incidentally, that he has retired from business and is 'a gentleman of considerable independent property' (Chapter 34). Although he often looks ridiculous when he is being helped over walls or pushed along in a wheelbarrow, being fat and always wearing those gaiters, he is remarkably sprightly for a man of his age. He also seems to have a surplus of emotional energy. His eyes twinkle behind his spectacles, as he beams benevolently on the world, and his rotundity, unlike that of Joe, the fat boy, only seems to emphasise that he has more money than he will ever need and is willing to endow others with the wherewithal to improve their lot, if they prove worthy of his patronage. When he feels, he feels deeply, as in the Fleet, for example, when his heart is 'really too full to bear' the sight of an unhappy family, and he retires early to bed (Chapter 41). He eats and drinks heavily most evenings, but almost invariably wakes up refreshed, as if renewed by sleep, like a child.

His own prosperity and innocence have hitherto protected him from the harsh realities of life, but his experiences in the novel, and particularly during his imprisonment, bring out the best in him. Early in the novel he proves to be an indifferent leader, who often needs rescuing from some predicament into which he has got himself, and who loses his temper often enough to be called 'old Fireworks' by Jingle (Chapter 20). His handling of Bob Sawyer, Ben Allen and his aunt, after his release from the Fleet, is characterised by a statesmanlike tact which indicates that he has a new authority, founded on experience. Dickens's own comments on Pickwick's character in the preface of the Charles Dickens edition (1867) are revealing. He implies that Pickwick is in one sense always the same, and that what actually changes is our own view of him:

> It has been observed of Mr Pickwick, that there is a decided change in his character, as these pages proceed, and that he becomes more good and more sensible. I do not think this change will appear forced or unnatural to my readers, if they will reflect that in real life the peculiarities and oddities of a man who has anything whimsical about him, generally impress us first, and that it is not until we are better acquainted with him that we usually begin to look below these superficial traits, and to know the better part of him.

The very fact that we know so little about Pickwick's life before his retirement adds to the impression that he is, as it were, 'born' at the beginning of the novel, as he bursts 'like another sun from his slumbers' on the morning of 30 May 1827, and sets off 'with his portmanteau in his hand, his telescope in his great-coat pocket, and his note-book in his waistcoat' (Chapter 2). Apparently reborn every morning, and at once old and young, wise and foolish, protective and vulnerable, Pickwick is indeed in a sense 'immortal', as he is jocularly described in the very first chapter.

Nathaniel Winkle

In his 1867 preface, Dickens states that he 'put in Mr Winkle expressly for the use of MR SEYMOUR', as the original plan was for him to supply the text to accompany Seymour's prints, illustrative of the difficulties into which members of a 'Nimrod Club' get themselves through their 'want of dexterity' at 'shooting, fishing, and so forth'. Thus the 'sporting Winkle' is introduced to us suitably dressed in 'a new green shooting coat, plaid neckerchief, and closely-fitted drabs' (Chapter 1). When it emerges that he is decidedly unskilled at riding, shooting and skating, Pickwick calls him a 'humbug', an 'impostor' (Chapter 30). Although Winkle matters less as the novel unfolds, Dickens introduces him more often than he does Snodgrass and Tupman. He proves to be a blunderer in other spheres too, as when he blurts out the incriminating evidence during Pickwick's trial, for example (Chapter 34).

Augustus Snodgrass

Like Winkle, the 'poetic Snodgrass' is dressed in clothes suited to the role he is to play in the early chapters of the novel: 'poetically enveloped in a mysterious blue coat with a canine-skin collar' (Chapter 1). His names epitomise the mock-heroic quality of that gap between appearance and reality mentioned earlier (see p.49). 'Augustus' evokes the great age of literary eminence under the Roman Emperor Augustus, and the 'Augustan' age of the eighteenth century in England, whereas 'Snodgrass' is a surname perhaps better suited to a provincial English tradesman. His language is as pseudo-poetic as his name. Consider his heroic description of the troops in the military review, whose eyes, the observant Pickwick notices, actually stare blankly forward, and hardly bespeak intelligence in their owners: 'It is indeed a noble and a brilliant sight . . . to see the gallant defenders of their country drawn up in brilliant array before its peaceful citizens . . . their eyes flashing—not with the rude fire of rapine or revenge, but with the soft light of humanity and intelligence' (Chapter 4). Snodgrass acts in character in the early chapters of the novel, whispering 'poetical sentiments' to Emily Wardle (Chapter 6), for example. But although Dickens occasionally uses him as a means by which to mock some of his own 'poetic' colleagues in the literary world, as at Mrs Hunter's literary breakfast, he soon fades from the centre of attention in the novel.

Tracy Tupman

In one sense the least significant of the Pickwickians, Tupman represents the most significant of the ruling passions among them: 'the too susceptible Tupman, who to the wisdom and experience of maturer years superadded the enthusiasm and ardour of a boy, in the most interesting and pardonable of human weaknesses—love' (Chapter 1). In the frontispiece to *Pickwick*, it is Tupman whose round face takes pride of place in the central shield beneath a picture of Pickwick and Sam. (Snodgrass and Winkle are one on each side of him, looking inwards.) He is of more interest symbolically than as a character in his own right. His romantic involvement with Miss Rachael Wardle proves to be no more than a comic interlude, from which he recovers with remarkable rapidity after her abortive elopement with Jingle. For the remainder of the novel, Tupman remains a rather inconsequential figure, notable only for his harmless silliness, as when he runs off shouting 'Fire!' on seeing Pickwick fall through the ice at Dingley Dell (Chapter 30).

Sam Weller

As they travel from Eatanswill to Bury St Edmunds, Sam tells Pickwick about his background (Chapter 16). First he was a carrier's boy, 'then a vagginer's, then a helper, then a boots'. When he ran away from the carrier, he spent two weeks underneath the dry arches of Waterloo Bridge, where he saw some 'queer sights', such as 'worn-out, starving, houseless creeturs', and child beggars. Whereas Pickwick, whose Christian name he shares, is old in years and yet childishly innocent, Sam is young enough to be his son, yet has far more experience of the hard world. Not only is he experienced and intelligent; he also has a remarkably forgiving nature, when we consider the lack of parental care implicit in that early pitching 'neck and crop into the world, to play at leap-frog with its troubles'. Far from seeking revenge on the older generation, like some of the sons who figure in the interpolated tales, Sam is a model son to his (again childlike) father, Tony, and surrogate son to Pickwick, for whom he *acts* when the master wills. Like Pickwick, although for quite different reasons, he embarks on his first tour with an easy-going and open view of its possibilities, simply being ready to see what turns up: 'there's change of air, plenty to see, and little to do; and all this suits my complaint uncommon' (Chapter 12). (We have already seen (p.47) that, as a servant, Sam provides a 'below stairs' parallel to Pickwick, his master.) He is adored by members of his own class, who respect him for his bluntness, his black humour, inherited from his father, and his frank, unservile behaviour towards his 'superiors'. He is the type of the free-born Englishman, in Dickens's eyes, unimpressed by superiority of rank or material possessions, but utterly loyal to those he respects for themselves. The very rapidity with which he makes up his mind and acts upon his decision, as when he hits people or knocks their hats off, for example, or when he threatens to sleep on the gravel at the Fleet, indicates an open nature and a quick intelligence which combine to make him as lovable as his 'immortal' master.

Themes

At first sight, *Pickwick Papers* seems one of the easiest of Dickens's novels to understand and to analyse critically, partly because Pickwick himself is not a complex character. The central theme of the novel, however, is actually quite difficult to grasp, with its religious overtones. We must tackle this theme in order to appreciate the order of Dickens's achievement in his first novel.

Love

The central theme of *Pickwick* is closely associated with its central character. Let us first consider the source and nature of Pickwick's innocence. The poet W.H. Auden (1907–73) wrote:

> The real theme of *Pickwick Papers*—I am not saying Dickens was consciously aware of it, and, indeed, I am pretty certain he was not— is the Fall of Man. It is the story of a man who is innocent, that is to say, who has not eaten of the Tree of the Knowledge of Good and Evil [Genesis 3] and is, therefore, living in Eden. He then eats of the Tree, that is to say, he becomes conscious of the reality of Evil but, instead of falling from innocence into sin—this is what makes him a mythical character—he changes from an innocent child into an innocent adult who no longer lives in an imaginary Eden of his own but in the real and fallen world.*

This view of the novel helps to explain how Pickwick seems to be reborn every day, as if untouched by the corruption of the fallen world. But Steven Marcus chooses a different religious analogy in order to explain how Pickwick engages with the real, fallen world. He claims that Dickens achieved 'transcendence' in his first novel, 'the very thing we tend to think is the exclusive right of only the greatest, most mature, most fully consummated artists'.† By transcendence he means 'a representation of life which fulfils that vision, which men have never yet relinquished, of the ideal possibilities of human relations in community'. The enduring universal popularity of *Pickwick*, he argues, is largely explained by the fact that no novel could move further 'toward asserting not only that the Kingdom of God is within each man but that it is possible to establish something that resembles the Kingdom of God on Earth'.‡ The Wellers, Marcus suggests, are 'tutelary spirits' in the 'mythical country' of the novel, who 'watch over Pickwick and keep him in touch with the solid earth'.§ (They also contribute to that comic dimension of the novel which prevents it from sliding into sentimentality.)

The concept of the Kingdom of God (or of Heaven) is notoriously difficult to understand or explain, and, indeed, Christ himself uses several quite different analogies in his gospel parables in order to explain it. One strand of Christian thought on the Kingdom is worth emphasising here, however, namely that there is a strong connection between 'Heaven' in the sense of a future state, after death, and the idea that the

---

*W.H. Auden, 'Dingley Dell & The Fleet', in *The Dyer's Hand and Other Essays*, Faber, London, 1963, pp.408–9.

†Steven Marcus, *Dickens: From Pickwick to Dombey*, p.17.

‡*Dickens: From Pickwick to Dombey*, p.51.

§*Dickens: From Pickwick to Dombey*, p.52.

Kingdom of God is all around us here on earth, as a potential state achieved through love: love of God and of our fellow men. We may only catch glimpses of this Kingdom on earth, but it is none the less vividly present to those who have eyes to see. It is as if in this life we are walking down a dark, wet city street, but occasionally we pass a house in which a party is going on, and from which pour warmth, light, and the sound of laughter.

As a Christian, Dickens certainly understood the larger significance of human love in a fallen world, and in *Pickwick* he made this his central theme. In the preface to the first book edition (1837), he wrote that if any of his 'imperfect descriptions' should 'induce only one reader to think better of his fellow men, and to look upon the brighter and more kindly side of human nature, he would indeed be proud and happy to have led to such a result'. We have seen that he tended to separate good from evil in the early chapters of the novel, by portraying the darker side of man's nature only in the interpolated tales. His characters are constantly shutting out the world, as it were, seeking out snug corners of public houses and warm domestic hearths, where good fellowship and shared food and drink warm the heart. Notice, however, that the grimmer interpolated tales are actually told within such snuggeries, thus heightening the contrast between the human fellowship within and the potential violence and hatred without. Many scenes in the novel are set in cosy, enclosed places. For example, Hablot Browne's plate called 'The Valentine' has the rotund Tony Weller standing in front of the fire in the Blue Boar, Leadenhall Market, smoking a long clay pipe, and Sam reading the valentine to him, seated at a homely table and separated from the rest of the room by a screen which adds to the sense of enclosure in the scene (Chapter 33). When Sam later attends the soirée of the Bath footmen, he is led through a greengrocer's shop to a small parlour at the back, where preparations have been made for dinner: 'Plates for a corresponding number of guests were warming behind the fender; and the guests themselves were warming before it . . .' (Chapter 37).

Similar scenes recur throughout the novel, but clearly the major ones are those at Dingley Dell. During the games of cards at Manor Farm, on the Pickwickians' first evening there, the 'benevolent clergyman' looks pleasantly on as the company joke and flirt together: 'for the happy faces which surrounded the table made the good old man feel happy too; and though the merriment was rather boisterous, still it came from the heart and not from the lips: and this is the right sort of merriment, after all' (Chapter 6). Dickens's comment on true *feeling* is highly significant in a novel in which domesticated human love is venerated in the spirit of William Wordsworth's (1770–1850) poem, 'Tintern Abbey' (1798):

> . . . feelings too
> Of unremembered pleasure: such, perhaps,
> As have no slight or trivial influence
> On that best portion of a good man's life,
> His little, nameless, unremembered, acts
> Of kindness and of love.   (lines 30–5)

Significantly, the old clergyman talks about the heart in 'The Convict's Return', his grim story of family breakdown: 'Heaven forgive me the supposition, if it be an uncharitable one, but I do firmly and in my soul believe, that the man systematically tried for many years to break her heart' (Chapter 6). Later in the novel, when introducing the Christmas scenes at Dingley Dell, Dickens writes of the 'pure and unalloyed delight' of family reunions, which Christians and non-Christians alike have seen as being 'among the first joys of a future condition of existence, provided for the blest and happy' (Chapter 28). This is a clear example of the connection between a future Heaven and the Kingdom of Heaven on earth. On Christmas Eve, Wardle tells the story on Gabriel Grub in the warm farmhouse, with snowdrifts and a piercingly cold wind firmly shut out. The Sexton at first reverses the Christmas scene at Dingley Dell, deliberately going outside to dig the grave, and thus avoiding his neighbours. His painful education at the hands of the goblins shows him that 'happiness, contentment, and peace' are achieved through love (Chapter 29).

In the Fleet, Pickwick puts the gospel message of brotherly love into practice, ministering to Jingle and Job Trotter, whose genuine tears indicate that they are in real need of help and comfort. Sam comments to Job: 'I never heerd, mind you, nor read of in story-books, nor see in picters, any angel in tights and gaiters—not even in spectacles . . . but mark my vords, Job Trotter, he's a reg'lar thorough-bred angel for all that' (Chapter 45). (Again, the humorous way Sam puts this saves the speech from sentimentality.) Perker recognises that Pickwick's benevolence towards Jingle and Job is real 'charity' (Chapter 53), the word from the Latin *caritas* which, in the Authorised Version of the Bible, is used to convey the meaning of the original Greek *agape*, love: 'And now abideth faith, hope, charity, these three; but the greatest of these is charity' (I Corinthians 13:13). The ethics of love in *Pickwick* are broadly based on the Beatitudes in the Bible ('Blessed are the meek: for they shall inherit the earth', . . . 'Blessed are the merciful: for they shall obtain mercy', Matthew 5) and Christ's words to his disciples concerning the Kingdom prepared for those who love their fellow men ('Naked, and ye clothed me . . . *in prison, and ye came unto me*', Matthew 25:36).

The New Testament sense of love is distinct from the kind of love between the sexes which is associated with the Greek word *eros*. This other kind of love interest in *Pickwick* is the main focus for Dickens's comic treatment of human *limitations*. Predatory widows haunt the novel, hysterical creatures who can 'force on' tears when it suits them (Chapter 27). (Notice how this contrasts with the clergyman's thoughts on true feeling.) Men are shown to be irresponsible in their flirtations and scheming in their pursuit of women merely for their money. Choose a few examples of Dickens's handling of true and false love between the sexes, and compare them with his treatment of Pickwick's love for his fellow human beings in the novel. What conclusions do you come to concerning Dickens's views on human nature?

England and English law

Pickwick's tours differ from those of most tourists in that he is much less concerned with visiting places of interest or discovering beautiful views than with meeting people. So this most English of English novels portrays a wide range of people at work and at play before the development of the railways and the consequent impact of industry on a formerly agricultural and trading nation. Pickwick can examine several different kinds of life. There is the life of the open road, with its turnpikes and hospitable coaching inns, and coachmen such as Tony Weller and his friends. The life of the country—of shooting, games of cricket and stories round the fire—is enjoyed by Wardle and his family. Provincial town life, with its snobbishness and pettiness across the social range, is represented in Bristol and Rochester, Eatanswill and Ipswich. Pickwick always returns to the life of London, with its public houses, its bachelor lodgings, and its dingy offices, until his final retirement to delightful Dulwich.

As Pickwick moves around the country, Dickens pokes fun at the English professions. Medicine is represented by young Bob Sawyer and his friend Bob Allen, church and chapel by the clergyman at Dingley Dell and the Reverend Mr Stiggins of Dorking, politics by the Honourable Samuel Slumkey, Member of Parliament elect for Eatanswill, and the army by Dr Slammer and his friends, and Mr Dowler. Dickens uses most of these characters to ridicule gently the pretensions and pomposity of the English professional classes.

Dickens's handling of the law is, of course, far less gentle. In this respect the seeds of some of his later novels can be seen in *Pickwick*. For example, the name of Mrs Bardell's lawyer, Fogg, points forward to the famous opening pages of *Bleak House*: 'Fog everywhere. Fog up the river . . . fog down the river . . . Fog on the Essex marshes, fog on the Kentish heights . . . And hard by Temple Bar, in Lincoln's Inn Hall, at the very heart of the fog, sits the Lord High Chancellor in his High Court of Chancery.' The smell of rottenness and decay which pervades *Bleak House* also has a precedent in *Pickwick*, where Dickens describes the lawyers' offices in the Temple, for example: 'They are, for the most part, low-roofed, mouldy rooms, where innumerable rolls of parchment, which have been perspiring in secret for the last century, send forth an agreeable odour, which is mingled by day with the scent of dry rot, and by night with the various exhalations which arise from damp cloaks, festering umbrellas, and the coarsest tallow candles' (Chapter 31). Serjeant Snubbin's 'sanctum', with a bookcase whose doors are 'rotting in their hinges' and with a carpet so filthy that dust flies out of it 'in little clouds at every step', is one of many such rooms in Dickens's novels, including Jaggers's sinister office in *Great Expectations*. Rottenness and decay symbolically suggest the corruption and deadness of the English legal system. (Perker 'disinters' his papers from his blue bag before the trial (Chapter 34).) The law is shown to be life-denying rather than life-affirming, so that we applaud Sam's vigorous defiance of the law officers he encounters, and his father's animated shouts from the gallery at Pickwick's trial. The darkest aspects of *Pickwick* are associated with the law, from the dreadful interpolated tale of 'The Queer Client', in which Heyling destroys his father-in-law, using the law as a weapon, to the 'poor side' of the Fleet prison, in which those who are imprisoned for debt suffer more than hardened criminals in other prisons, some of them actually starving to death (Chapter 42). The activities of the lawyers with whom Pickwick comes in contact, and the state of the prisoners in the Fleet, point to the shortcomings of the English legal and penal systems of the day. But Pickwick's heart directs him to love his neighbour. He thus acts in the spirit of the New Testament rather than in the law-bound tradition of the Old Testament. (St Paul writes to the Christians at Corinth: 'Ye are our epistle written in our hearts, known and read of all men: Forasmuch as ye are manifestly declared to be the epistle of Christ ministered by us, written not with ink, but with the Spirit of the living God; not in tables of stone, but in fleshy tables of the heart. . . . the letter killeth, but the spirit giveth life', II Corinthians 3:2–6.)

Part 4

Hints for study

Let us now assume that you have read *Pickwick* once, and have read at least parts of these Notes. How should you go about studying the novel in more detail, and specifically with possible examinations in mind? You must certainly be prepared to read parts of the novel again very carefully, although you may not find time to reread the whole of it. Perhaps the best way of organising your thoughts would be to write some short essays on particular aspects of the novel, or to write brief notes on specific questions. This would force you to select material for discussion and to get that material into some sort of order, which is excellent practice for the writing of examination answers. Here are six general points to consider when rereading the novel, and when writing essays or answering questions on it:

(1) *Critical reading:* There is a 'naive reader' in all of us, who gets involved in the story, finds characters interesting, and looks forward to learning what happens at the end of a novel. We must never lose this kind of involvement and interest. But we also have to develop the 'critical reader' in us who will, as it were, look over the shoulder of our more naive self and ask *why* we are interested, and *how* the writer has achieved his effects. So always consider form or technique as well as content or themes, and try to relate them.

(2) *Argument of an essay:* You should always try to argue a case in an essay or examination answer, based on *your* ideas, *your* views on the topic. You will often be asked a specific question, and can explain your point of view in answering it. If an examination 'question' does not actually ask you a question, but demands some kind of critical analysis from you, analyse the question and start asking yourself questions about it. (See first sample question below.)

(3) *Use of criticism:* Although it is not essential that you read large quantities of criticism, try to read at least some in the course of your studies, so that you can sharpen up your own ideas on *Pickwick* in relation to other people's ideas. (See 'Suggestions for further reading', below.) You may disagree with some of the things the critics say, and, indeed, this can be a good sign. If you wish, bring occasional references to or quotations from critics into your essays, and argue for or against their views. This will help you to make your essay lively and argumentative rather than dull and passive. But never read criticism as a substitute for reading the literary text itself.

(4) *Detailed examples:* Whatever your broad views on a question happen to be, always go back to the novel and reread those pages which you think are crucial from your particular point of view. Try to find some small passages, or even a few words, which perfectly illustrate the point you want to make, and either quote them or refer to them in your essay, adding your own critical comments and linking them to your main argument.

(5) *Generalisations and summaries:* Be very careful when making broad generalisations, as they so often turn out to be only half-truths. If you do generalise, always substantiate your broad points with specific examples. Never summarise at length. You can assume that the reader of what you write (teacher or examiner) knows the text to which you are referring. Therefore you should not waste valuable time and space writing a plot summary for him. Rather, refer only to those parts of the novel which you think are significant, as you would to a fellow student who also knows the novel well. Above all, do not try to summarise parts of the novel which are not relevant to the particular question you are tackling. You must *answer the question.*

(6) *Essay plans:* Before starting to write an essay or an examination answer, jot down the subjects of each paragraph in heading form. Then stick to your plan as you write the essay or answer.

Let us now take a number of questions of the kind which you might work on with your teacher or answer in examinations. You will see that the first question is followed by an essay plan, indicating just one of several ways in which one might tackle the question. Notice that the headings (in italics) should remind you of what you wanted to write about in each paragraph. Your essay plan could simply consist of these headings, perhaps followed by very *brief* references to the material you have selected for discussion. The material in brackets in the first specimen answer indicates the kind of argument and pieces of evidence which you might introduce in each paragraph of the essay proper.

Some possible questions

(1) *Examine the character and role of Sam Weller*

(*a*) *Character/role?* (Outline what you think the question means: distinctions between Sam's personality, behaviour, and so on, and his functions in the novel, as Pickwick's servant, of course, but also as his surrogate son, who knows more about the world than he does.)

(*b*) *What kind of man?* (As a way into this first part of the question, perhaps focus on Chapter 10, in which Sam is introduced: (i) refer to his cheeky exchanges with the chambermaid and his first black joke, about the hangman (quote this?); (ii) show how his discussion with

Jingle reveals that he is a man of the world; (iii) quote the part of the opening exchange between Sam and Perker in which Sam replies to Perker's comment on this 'curious old house'.)

(c) *Expand on* (b) (From the first, as we saw in (b), Sam is nimble-witted, self-confident, and unservile in his attitude towards his social 'superiors'. Now illustrate how he proves his loyalty to Pickwick and to his father, Tony, through a series of incidents and encounters later in the novel. Use examples of the kind chosen in the 'Characterisation' section of Part 3, 'Commentary'. You may need two or three paragraphs on this.)

(d) *What role does he have in society?* (Again return to Chapter 10 for your first detailed example. Quote the sentence in which Dickens describes how Sam's old white hat is '*carelessly* thrown on one side of his head', and comment on how Sam fulfils the role of 'boots' in a *carefree* manner. Then you might refer to his change of clothes when he becomes Pickwick's servant, and thus changes roles (Chapter 12), and quote his own thoughts on the vagueness of his new role: 'I wonder whether I'm meant to be a footman, or a groom, or a gamekeeper, or a seedsman. I looks like a sort of compo of every one on 'em . . .' (Chapter 12).)

(e) *Below stairs* (Sam's life 'below stairs' as a servant parallels his master's life in several respects (see p.47). Note how popular he is with fellow members of the servant class.)

(f) *His role in relation to Pickwick* (Sam's hard upbringing (Chapter 16) has taught him more about the world than his much older but innocent master knows. Thus Sam is also a foil to Pickwick, providing interesting *contrasts*. Refer, for example, to Hablot Browne's plate of their first meeting at the White Hart Inn (Chapter 10), in which the illustrator contrasts the two thin men on the left (Sam and Perker) with the two fat men on the right (Wardle and Pickwick). Develop this briefly by again touching on Sam's relationship with his fat father, Tony. Then quote Steven Marcus's comments on the role of the Wellers as 'the geniuses of the mythical country of *Pickwick Papers*, tutelary spirits who watch over Pickwick and keep him in touch with the solid earth'.* Expand on this, and see 'Themes' in Part 3.)

(g) *Conclusion* (Sam Weller, who is as important as Pickwick in the novel, is probably also the most interesting character. His energy, his good-humoured approach to his 'betters', and his loyalty, all make him attractive. Above all, there is little or no conflict between his character and his role, for he is always irrepressibly himself. A servant, he is the freest man in the novel. A member of the lower orders, he is somehow classless.)

*Steven Marcus, *Dickens: From Pickwick to Dombey*, p.52.

(2) *To what extent do you consider that Dickens explores serious themes in his comic novel?*

What does 'comic novel' mean? There are two possible meanings: a novel which ends happily (as opposed to a tragic novel), or a novel which portrays the world from comic 'angles', and is full of humorous incidents. *Pickwick* is a comic novel in both senses. The early numbers read like a comic miscellany. (Illustrate with examples.) But the dark interpolated tales are important. (Examples.) As the Bardell plot and the attack on the law develop, the novel itself darkens. (Refer particularly to the Fleet chapters.) The major theme in the novel is of Christian brotherly love, and the happy ending is made possible only through Pickwick's personal suffering and his constant benevolence to those less fortunate than himself. Thus by portraying the lovable Pickwick getting himself into all kinds of comic predicaments, as well as by showing how, for example, the selfish Jingle ends up in the 'poor side' of the Fleet, Dickens is actually saying something deeply serious about human priorities in a potentially hard world. His comic vision enables him to portray the better sides of human nature without sentimentality.

(3) *Write a critical account of Chapter 47, commenting on its function in the novel*

As this is the last of the chapters devoted to Pickwick's imprisonment in the Fleet, comment on the significance of the Fleet chapters in general before concentrating on Chapter 47 in particular. (Perhaps read Auden on 'Dingley Dell & The Fleet' and quote him on Pickwick's innocence in a fallen world.) Then consider the function of Chapter 47 in terms of plot, for it is here that many of the sub-plots of the middle part of *Pickwick* are drawn together as different characters arrive in the prison, either as inmates or as visitors. Mrs Bardell's arrival at the end of the previous chapter has led Sam to send Job Trotter to inform Perker. This Job does at the beginning of Chapter 47. Next morning, Perker exerts pressure on Pickwick to settle with Dodson and Fogg for the sake of Mrs Bardell, as well as for his own. Comment on the way in which this pressure is increased by the (coincidental?) arrival of Winkle with his new wife, Arabella, who also need Pickwick's help, and can benefit by it only if he leaves the prison. Tupman's and Snodgrass's arrival, and the manner in which Pickwick and Sam leave the Fleet, still acting benevolently towards their fellow prisoners, should be briefly mentioned. Finally, review the chapter as a whole, and point out how Pickwick has accumulated responsibilities in the course of the novel, and now in the Fleet has taken the suffering and problems of others on his own shoulders.

---

(4) *With close reference to a few examples, illustrate how Dickens reveals the characteristics of professional groups and individual people through the language they use*

Reread the section on Dickens's comic style in 'Style and narrative technique' (pp.48–50), and examine the passages referred to there (in Chapters 1, 15 and 34) where parliamentary style, newspaper style and courtroom style are parodied. Concentrating on these three styles, examine a few sentences of each in detail, saying what you think they reveal both about the professions and about the individuals in each case, and commenting on how Dickens achieves his effects. Then move on to idiosyncratic styles such as Jingle's, and comment on Dickens's use of exaggeration for comic effect. Discuss the characteristics of Jingle which are reflected in his style of speech. Choose perhaps one other example of this kind. End with some general conclusion, firmly based on your detailed examples, concerning the flexibility and energy of Dickens's language in the novel, and particularly of the styles of speech of some of his characters.

Further sample questions

Write brief notes, with headings, on each of the following questions, and then expand some of these notes into fully-fledged essays, always illustrating your answers with detailed references to the novel.
(1) What is the significance of Dickens's comic treatment of the Reverend Mr Stiggins in the context of the novel as a whole?
(2) To what extent can the number of minor characters in the novel be justified?
(3) Analyse 'The Story of the Goblins who stole a Sexton' (Chapter 29), and explain why you think it is important in the context of Christmas at Dingley Dell.
(4) Compare and contrast Dickens's organisation of his material in one of the early and one of the later serial numbers.*
(5) Discuss Dickens's treatment of the law.
(6) Discuss some of the ways in which Dickens introduces his characters to the reader.
(7) 'As it grew into a novel, *Pickwick* did not lose its character as a miscellany . . . nor its loosely picaresque form' (Butt and Tillotson). Discuss.
(8) Does Pickwick change, or appear to change, during the course of the novel? If so, in what way(s)?

*The monthly number divisions are given in roman numerals in the General summary, Part 2.

Part 5

Suggestions for further reading

The text

The most useful modern edition is in the Penguin English Library, edited by Robert L. Patten, Penguin Books, Harmondsworth, 1972.

Other works by Dickens

Dickens's other novels are listed in the biographical section of Part 1, 'Introduction'. If possible you should read one or more of these, perhaps concentrating on the maturer novels, which will provide a contrast to *Pickwick*. *Great Expectations* is one of the most fascinating mature novels, without being the most elaborate in structure and scope (its themes of love, the law and so on can also be related to those of *Pickwick* in some respects).

Correspondence
HOUSE, MADELINE, STOREY, GRAHAM, ET AL. (EDS.): *The Letters of Charles Dickens*, 4 vols published to date, Pilgrim Edition, Clarendon Press, Oxford, 1965–. The period of *Pickwick* is covered in vol. 1 (1820–39)

Background, biography and general works on Dickens

Background
HOUSE, HUMPHRY: *The Dickens World*, Oxford University Press, London, 1941. This book places Dickens and his fiction in their historical context
WILSON, ANGUS: *The World of Charles Dickens*, Secker and Warburg, London, 1970. A lively, personal, lavishly illustrated account of Dickens's life, work and times
Biography
FORSTER, JOHN: *The Life of Charles Dickens*, ed. A.J. Hoppé, 2 vols, Dent, London, 1966. The famous, very long biography by Dickens's friend and literary adviser, first published in 1872–4
JOHNSON, EDGAR: *Charles Dickens: His Tragedy and Triumph*, 2 vols, Gollancz, London, 1953. A well written, scholarly biography. An abridged version is also available, Allen Lane, Harmondsworth, 1978

General introductions
FIELDING, K.J.: *Charles Dickens: A Critical Introduction*, Longman, London, 1958
JOHNSON, E.D.H.: *Charles Dickens: An Introduction to his Novels*, Random House, New York, 1969
MILLER, J. HILLIS: *Charles Dickens: The World of his Novels*, Harvard University Press, Cambridge, Massachusetts, 1958

Studies particularly useful for the student of *Pickwick*

BUTT, JOHN AND TILLOTSON, KATHLEEN: *Dickens at Work*, Methuen, London, 1957. Chapter III is an account of the planning and writing of *Pickwick* as a serial novel
KILLHAM, JOHN: '*Pickwick*, Dickens and the Art of Fiction', in *Dickens and the Twentieth Century*, ed. John Gross and Gabriel Pearson, Routledge and Kegan Paul, London, 1962, pp.35-47. Interesting on story, plot and character in *Pickwick*
AUDEN, W.H.: 'Dingley Dell & The Fleet', *The Dyer's Hand and Other Essays*, Faber, London, 1963. A mythic approach to the subject of innocence in *Pickwick*
MARCUS, STEVEN: *Dickens: From Pickwick to Dombey*, Chatto and Windus, London, 1965. This opens with a fascinating study of *Pickwick* ('The Blest Dawn') to which all later readers and critics are indebted
PATTEN, ROBERT L.: 'The Art of *Pickwick*'s Interpolated Tales', *English Literary History*, 34, 1967, pp.349-66. An informative study of the tales and their place in the novel as a whole

The author of these notes

DR MICHAEL WHEELER was educated at Magdalene College, Cambridge, and University College, London, where he also taught for a year as Quain Student. Since 1973 he has been a Lecturer in English Literature at the University of Lancaster. His publications include a number of articles on Victorian literature and a book entitled *The Art of Allusion in Victorian Fiction* (1979).